Embroidery for Fashion

Embroidery for Fashion

Gisela Banbury and
Angela Dewar

B.T. Batsford Ltd London

First published 1985
© Gisela Banbury and Angela Dewar 1985

ISBN 0 7134 4266 2

Typeset by Tek-Art Ltd, Kent
and printed in Great Britain by
Anchor-Brendon Ltd.
Tiptree, Essex
for the publishers
B.T. Batsford Ltd
4 Fitzhardinge Street
London W1H 0AH

CONTENTS

ACKNOWLEDGMENTS

We would like to thank all the friends and members of The Embroiderers' Guild who lent us work and photographs. Our grateful thanks also to our models: Louise Coleman, Rosalind and Isabelle Dewar, Sarah and Ruth Gosling, Julie-Anne Greenslade, Alden Sellars and Uta Vian-Smith, and to Helen Dewar for her help with the index and typing.

The black and white photographs are by Brian McNeill, except for the following: figs 17, 23, 55, 58, 59, 64, 98, 122 (Tony Bader); figs 10, 97, 108 (Granville Davies); fig. 93 (Ken Grant); figs 31, 95 (Peter Haines); figs 88, 124, 130 (by courtesy of Medway College); fig. 73 (by courtesy of the National Portrait Gallery); fig. 92 (by courtesy of Anna Roose); fig. 81 (Jennifer Stuart).

The Colour photographs are by Tony Bader. The diagrams are by Gisela Banbury. The line drawings are by Pat Gillam, except for the following: fig. 89 (Gisela Banbury); figs 57, 60, 61, 62, 90, 132 (Louise Coleman); figs 26, 40, 41, 85 (Angela Dewar); figs 12, 19, 32, 100, 116 (Frank Stark).

INTRODUCTION

If asked why they wear clothes, most people would answer: firstly, for comfort and protection, and, secondly, out of modesty. But these two reasons do not explain the time, skill and ingenuity mankind has spent on decorating garments from the earliest times.

It would be very simple and cheap for the textile industry to supply us with a kind of utilitarian cover-up to keep us physically and morally protected, but without doubt it would be a financial disaster. We do not just want to be comfortable and modest, we also want to look pretty, neat, attractive and elegant. We want our clothes to be 'fashionable', to show us 'in the best light', to make 'a good impression'. Clothes can also give an onlooker an insight into one's character.

Fashion dictates to a large extent the overall appearance of clothes, even for men and women who say they do not care about it. The grey-suited armies of commuters leaving for the city stations every morning confirm this. On close inspection, the great variety of ties worn by the men show a yearning for individuality. Any parent who ever watched a son or daughter personalizing a pair of jeans or T-shirt with bleaches, dyes, studs and patches knows that the loudly proclaimed uniformity, informality and equality in teenage dress does not exist.

We all like to conform to some extent, but are very pleased to be able to add a personal note to our dress and no other skill is more suited to achieving this than embroidery.

Thankfully, the times when law and social standing dictated the style of decoration on costume are gone. Today the only guidelines are taste and practicality, the only limit, one's skills. The purpose of this book is to guide you in the former and help you to develop the latter.

We have tried to show how embroidery can be used to decorate everyday clothes as well as garments for more formal occasions. During the middle years of this century, embroidery was confined mainly to use on evening wear, but this has not always been the case, as a study of historical costume reveals. Since 1980 there has been a marked increase in the use of embroidery on day wear. Many embroidered garments have been imported, especially from India, and although the embroidery is not always of a high standard, this has helped to promote the idea of decorated clothes for everyday use.

We have tried to include photographs and drawings of a range of garments and have given instructions for making some of them.

Throughout the book we have assumed that the reader has a basic knowledge of dressmaking methods and how to adapt them. Although fashion changes its shapes and textures frequently, design principles will always remain the same and should be applied to whichever style is being worn at any particular moment.

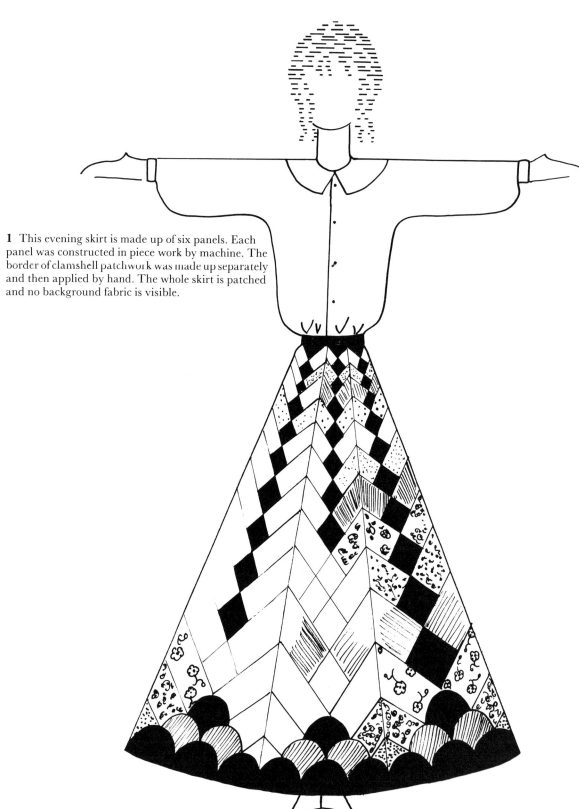

1 This evening skirt is made up of six panels. Each panel was constructed in piece work by machine. The border of clamshell patchwork was made up separately and then applied by hand. The whole skirt is patched and no background fabric is visible.

1 Materials and tools

Embroidery can be added to a garment at different stages. It can be worked onto the fabric before cutting out, onto the pattern pieces after cutting out, or onto the finished costume. Some garments, for example a lace dress or a patchwork skirt, are made up entirely from decoration without a background fabric. At whatever stage the embroidery is worked and whichever technique is used, it always becomes a permanent part of the garment. This fact has to be considered from the very beginning.

When choosing a design, technique and materials, remember that the embroidery will have to be cared for in the same way as the dress. They will have to be washed, ironed or dry-cleaned together. Therefore it is not advisable to decorate a garment with threads which will not tolerate the washing or ironing temperatures needed for the dress fabric. This does not mean that embroidery should always be worked in a thread spun from the same fibre as used in the dress fabric – linen on linen or silk on silk etc. It is never a mistake to follow this rule, but it would leave a very limited and dull choice. Many fibres are compatible. The care they require is similar to that needed for others and therefore they can be mixed.

Care of fabrics

The care of fabrics used in dressmaking is determined not only by the fibre used in their manufacture, but also by the many different finishing processes applied to improve their handling properties. This makes it difficult to know how to clean them. The Home Laundering Consultative Council of Great Britain (H.L.C.C.) issues coded care labels which should be supplied with fabric bought by the metre or yard and should be sewn into finished garments. This code is based on four symbols giving instructions on washing, bleaching, ironing and dry cleaning. The most important symbols for

the embroiderer who wants to find suitable embroidery threads to go with a particular fabric are the washtub and the iron. When looking after a garment which is made up from more than one kind of material, always treat it according to the needs of the weakest, and make sure fabrics and threads are colourfast.

Embroidery threads

Embroidery threads are not coded in the same way as fabrics, but they can easily be divided into categories according to the basic fibre used in their manufacture. The following embroidery threads are suitable for use on clothes:

'Linen' threads, as used for lacemaking, crochet and whitework, which are made from flax. White linen will stay white if it is boiled occasionally. It will stand up to high temperatures in washing and ironing.

Sewing cotton, stranded cotton, coton à broder, coton perlé, which are used for surface stitchery, blackwork, quilting, smocking, machine embroidery and patchwork. These are made from cotton and should be colourfast. Cotton, like linen, will tolerate high washing and ironing temperatures.

 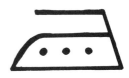

2 Symbols giving washing instructions for textiles. The washtub gives the number of the correct washing programme above the water line and the highest water temperature, in centigrade, below. Three dots on the iron indicate a hot iron and one dot a cool iron. Do not iron if this symbol is crossed out.

Silk threads, which are made from the filament of the silkworm and need much gentler treatment than linen and cotton. Washing temperatures should be no higher than 40°C and only a warm iron is required. Silk is soft, smooth and light.

Tapestry, crewel and knitting wools, which are spun from the fleece of animals such as sheep, goat, camel, hare etc. Like silk they should not be washed any hotter than 40°C. Wools are rougher and heavier than silk, and also not as strong.

Rayon threads, which are often used in machine embroidery and are also suitable for hand stitching. They are made from manmade regenerated fibres. They can be washed at 60°C but only require a warm iron. They are usually shiny and can be very thin.

Polyester and cotton-polyester sewing threads, which are often used in machine embroidery, machine quilting and patchwork. They are sold as multi-purpose threads and can be used on all fabrics. However, these threads are very hard and if applied in quantity they tend to stiffen the background fabric. They should not be ironed at a hot temperature.

Metal-look threads, which are on the market in a number of metallic colours and are used for machine embroidery. They are made of either rayon or polyester and should be treated accordingly. The type of threads traditionally used in goldwork are not really suitable for dress embroidery but can be used for accessories.

Tools and equipment

The tools and equipment required for fashion embroidery are much the same as those for dressmaking, with one or two additions. The following list includes several items which are not essential for making embroidered clothes, but may be useful:

Sewing machine. It is always advisable to buy the best machine that can be afforded. This does not necessarily mean a new machine, as a second-hand one of a good make can often be a better buy than an inferior new one. For some kinds of machine embroidery a straight-stitch machine is adequate. For zigzag stitching, a swing-needle machine is required and for automatic embroidery stitches, an even more sophisticated model. There are many machines on the market

to suit most pockets, but it is worth pointing out that the collar in figure 46 on page 53 was recently made on an old treddle machine.

Scissors. Several pairs are needed: large shears for cutting out fabrics; a pair of embroidery scissors; and a pair of very sharp, curved nail scissors. A pair of pinking shears can also be useful for making decorative effects on felts, leathers and suede (see figure 17, page 27).

Pins. Buy a box of good quality, steel pins and a pin cushion to stick them in. Long, glass-headed pins are more expensive, but easy to use.

Needles. The correct needle for the job is vital and Figure 3 shows part of an explanatory chart, issued by Henry Milward & Sons Limited of Studley, Warwickshire. A variety of machine needles is also available, in a number of sizes, with plain tips or ball ends and for sewing leather.

---

3 Part of an explanatory chart, issued by Henry Milward & Sons Limited, showing the correct needle for different purposes:

(a) *Glovers/Leather*
Leather needles have triangular points that pierce without tearing. Use them for gloves, belts and all garments in leather, vinyl or plastic.

(b) *Beading*
Beading needles are very fine and straight with long eyes. They are specially made to thread beads and pearls.

(c) *Ball point sewing*
Ball point needles are specially designed for use on jersey, stretch and other synthetic fabrics.

(d) *Sharps*
Sharps needles are for general purpose sewing. Their short round eyes provide added strength.

(e) *Tapestry*
Tapestry needles have blunt points which slip between fabric yarns without splitting them. Use them with wool or thick embroidery cotton on canvas or open-mesh fabric.

(f) *Embroidery/Crewel*
Embroidery or crewel needles are the same as sharps but have long eyes to take one or more threads of stranded cotton. Mainly used for embroidery.

(g) *Betweens/Quilting*
Betweens or quilting needles are short for quick, even stitching. Traditionally used by tailors and professional sewers.

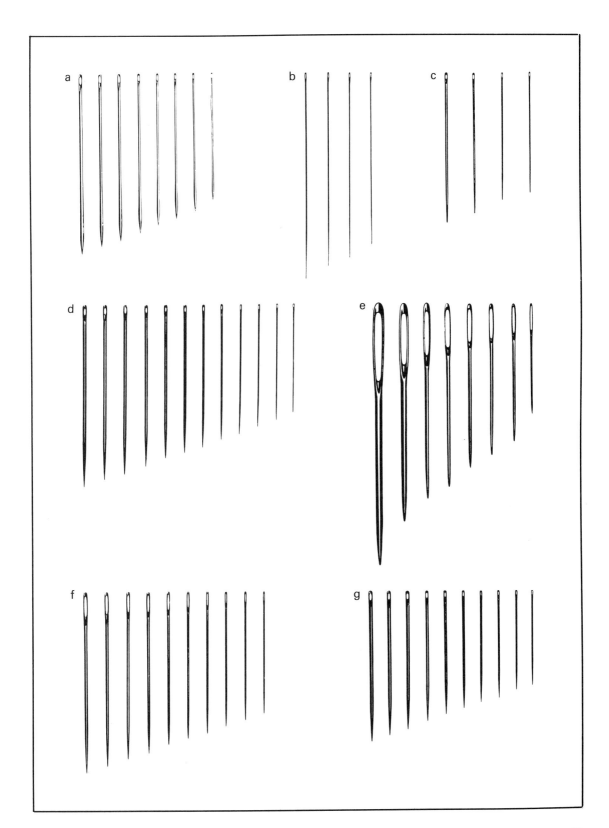

Seam ripper. To be used with caution!

Tape measure.

Screwdriver. This is usually one of the accessories for a sewing machine but is also useful for tightening up the rings of tambour frames.

Emery board. This is useful for smoothing broken nails or rough skin, both very inconvenient for sewing. Keep one near the work in progress.

Iron and ironing board. A steam iron is most useful. If this is not available, a small bowl of water and a pressing cloth of folded cheesecloth should be kept near the working area. It is wise to use the pressing cloth at all times, even when dry pressing. The surface of the ironing board or table should always be clean and smooth. A sleeve board and a tailor's 'ham' are both useful for pressing intricate parts of a garment, as well as sleeves. The ham is good for steam pressing curved areas when tailoring. A good substitute for a ham is a clean cloth, folded into a thick pad.

Embroidery frames

Embroidery techniques which require the needle to go in and out of the fabric in one movement, e.g. drawn thread work, patchwork and smocking, are best worked in the hand. Most other techniques, especially when worked over a large area, are improved if worked with the fabric either supported by a stiff backing (e.g. for insertions), or being held taut in an embroidery frame.

There are two basic types of embroidery frame: the round or tambour frame and the square or slate frame. Both types can be obtained in a variety of sizes and in more elaborate forms – table models, free-standing floor models, or quilting frames. For most needs, a 23 cm (9 in.) tambour frame and a simple slate frame are adequate.

Tambour frame

The tambour frame is probably the most useful frame for fashion embroidery. It is indispensable for free-machine embroidery and useful for linen embroidery such as pulled work, blackwork and cutwork. Heavily textured embroidery should not be worked in a tambour frame unless the embroidered area is small enough to fit within the circumference. The frame consists of two rings; the inner ring should be bound with bias binding

which prevents the frame from marking the fabric and stops the fabric slipping, the outer ring should have a screw which can be tightened. For machine embroidery the fabric *must* be stretched extremely tightly in the frame to avoid the stitches 'jumping'.

A tambour frame can be used for very small pieces of English quilting, such as a pocket. Stretch the backing fabric only into the frame to make the quilting puff up well.

Slate frame

The slate or square frame consists of two wooden rollers or rails, with a length of webbing fixed to them and two flat side pieces or stretchers, which have holes and pegs for stretching the fabric. A tapestry frame will have threaded, round stretchers with four wooden or plastic nuts on each side for tightening the material (*4*).

To dress a slate frame:

1 Measure the length of the webbing and mark the exact centre point with indelible ink.

2 Stitch tape down the sides of the fabric and turn under a hem at the top and bottom.

3 Mark the exact centre of the hems. Match each centre to the centre of the webbing and oversew

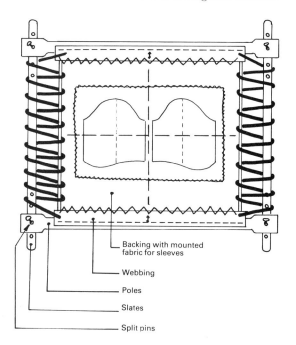

Backing with mounted
fabric for sleeves

Webbing

Poles

Slates

Split pins

4 A slate frame, dressed and with a pair of sleeves mounted ready for embroidery.

the fabric to the webbing, stitching from the centre outwards each time.

4 Take up the excess fabric by winding it around the rails, insert the stretchers and adjust the tension.

5 Each side of the fabric must now be laced to the stretchers, through the tape. Use string for this and begin at one end, leaving the excess string wound around the peg at the other. Lace each side before tightening both sides to produce an even tension. Wind the excess string around the pegs, or on a tapestry frame, around the stretchers.

When using a slate frame for English quilting, only the backing fabric should be stretched tightly into the frame. The top fabric should be tacked onto the filling and backing as described on page 60, leaving enough of the backing free to be fixed into the frame. This will allow the quilted pattern to stand out well.

To enlarge or reduce a design

Having chosen a design, it is often necessary to enlarge or reduce the size. First, take a tracing of the design onto a square piece of paper. Divide this square into four. This can be done by careful folding. Repeat several times until the tracing is divided into small, even squares.

Draw a second square of the size required for the finished embroidery. Divide this into exactly the same number of squares as the first. Mark each grid along the top and side with letters and numbers. Draw the design onto the second grid, square by square (5).

Transferring designs to fabrics

There are several orthodox ways of marking embroidery designs onto fabric. Three of them are given below and also a quicker method which is simple to use.

5 A design fitted into a grid, to be enlarged or reduced.

13

Trace tacking

This is suitable for fine fabrics and for marking the curved areas in counted thread designs.

1 Make a tracing of the design.

2 Pin and tack the tracing to the fabric.

3 Stitch around the entire design with small running stitches, taking care to begin and finish securely.

4 Gently tear away the tracing paper.

When working with this method, unpick approximately 1 cm ($\frac{1}{2}$ in.) at a time of the trace tacking as the embroidery progresses, otherwise it will be in the way.

Prick and pounce

This is suitable for all embroidery techniques where the surface stitchery will cover the marking.

1 Make a tracing of the design.

2 Closely prick the outlines of the design with a needle point (insert the blunt end into a cork to make it easier to hold).

3 Make up some pounce powder with ground charcoal and a little talcum powder.

4 Take a piece of felt or towelling approximately 8 cm ($3\frac{1}{4}$ in.) by 3 cm ($1\frac{1}{4}$ in.). Roll it up and stitch it into a tight pad.

5 Pin the pricked tracing rough side down onto the embroidery fabric and lay it onto a flat surface. It can be pinned onto a drawing board to hold it steady. (Pin through the outer edges of the spare cloth.)

6 Shake a little pounce powder onto the tracing and gently work it into the holes with the pad, using a circular motion.

7 When all the design has been pounced, remove the tracing very carefully.

8 With a fine brush and some watercolour or poster paint, paint the outline of the design onto the fabric. Use the most suitable colour for the background material. The pounce powder can be shaken off when the paint is dry.

Trace and mark

This is suitable for embroidery on sheer or transparent fabrics.

1 Make a bold tracing of the design.

2 Pin the tracing to a drawing board and lay the embroidery fabric over it. It can be pinned to keep it steady.

3 Using watercolour paint, or a water-soluble marker pen (see Suppliers', page 142) trace the design onto the fabric. Remove when dry.

Window tracing

This is suitable for all kinds of embroidery, even quite large pieces, except on very heavy or thick fabrics.

1 Make a tracing of the design.

2 Tape the tracing onto a large window which has a good light behind it.

3 Using a putty-type adhesive, fix the embroidery fabric over the tracing in the correct position.

4 Mark the design onto the fabric with a water-soluble marker pen.

This method is suitable for canvas work, but use an indelible marker or waterproof paint, as the work frequently requires dampening on completion and the colours may run into the embroidery.

2 Seams

Embroidery along seam lines

Most clothes are cut from flat-lying fabrics – pattern pieces are cut and seamed together to make up a garment. The most common seam in dressmaking is the open seam, in which two pattern pieces are placed right sides together and joined along the stitch line using a straight stitch on the sewing machine. The two seam allowances on the reverse side of the garment are opened out and pressed. On the right side of the garment only a neat, thin line is visible, either straight or curved, as the dress pattern dictates.

The seam line can be used as a guide for embroidery to be placed on the garment. Sometimes seams are introduced to a pattern specifically for this particular purpose (6). The embroidery can be worked by hand or machine. It can be placed on one or both sides of the seam line, very close to it or further away. It can go over the seam to cover it up as on the raglan sleeve (7). To make sure that the seam allowances do not move and pucker when the embroidery is added, it is advisable to tack them into place. All curved seams must be snipped to make them lie flat.

With a sewing machine it is very easy and quick to add some decorative stitches along a seam line. A row of straight stitches in a contrasting colour can immediately give a personal note to a simple garment. Modern machines often have a number of automatic embroidery stitches built in, from simple zigzag to complicated overlocking stitches, which can be used by themselves or in conjunction with each other, or combined with some hand stitching (8).

Interchange of colours

Where two pieces of fabric of different tone value are joined together a very hard line is created. If this sudden change is unwanted it can be softened with a colour interchange, when stitches in the opposing colour are worked along opposite sides of the seam line, as shown in figure 8. These decorations do not have to be very elaborate. They might simply be seeded stitches, rows of surface stitches or automatic machine stitches. Applied ribbons and cords of different widths in the two colours will have the same softening effect.

Somerset patchwork

Somerset patchwork consists of a number of fabric squares folded into triangles. These are usually arranged in a circle or square and sewn by hand onto a background fabric. Worked in this way it is not as hardwearing as many other types of patchwork and therefore is not very suitable for fashion items, but when adapted it makes attractive decorations along seams and edges, and can even be built up into wide borders.

Somerset triangles or points can be sewn into any seam, straight or curved (10). The points are made up individually as follows:

1 To make a finished point measuring 4 cm (1½ in.) along the seam line and 2 cm (¾ in.) from the seam to its highest point, cut a fabric square measuring 6 cm (2½ in.) by 6 cm (2½ in.). (This will leave a seam allowance of 1 cm (½ in.).)

2 Place the fabric square on the table wrong side up.

3 Fold the square in half horizontally, wrong sides together.

4 Mark the centre of the lower side of the oblong and bring the two folded upper corners down to meet at this point.

5 Press gently and make sure that the two folded edges make a neat slit along the centre line and come to a sharp point at the top. Hold the triangles in shape with a pin.

Make up the required number of Somerset points in this way. Arrange the triangles along the seam or edge to be decorated, with the folded side

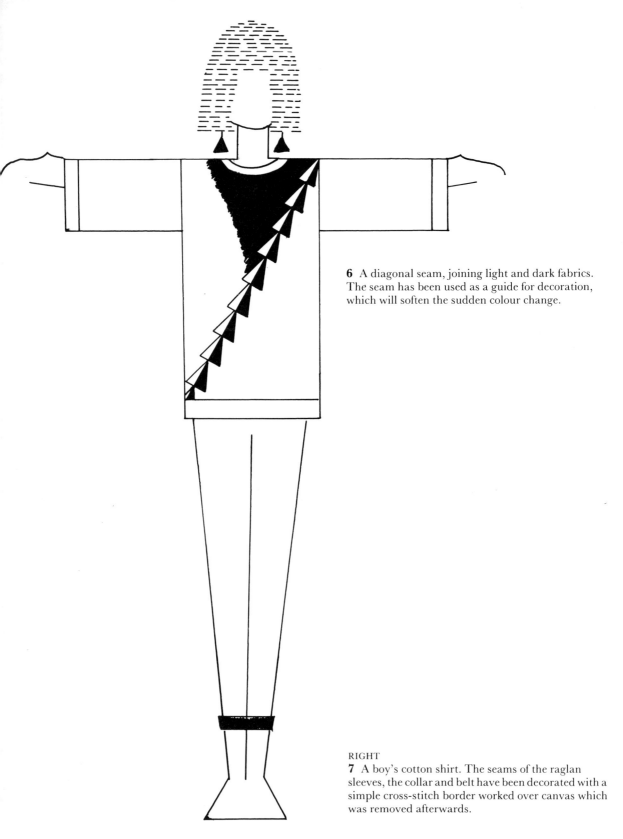

6 A diagonal seam, joining light and dark fabrics. The seam has been used as a guide for decoration, which will soften the sudden colour change.

RIGHT
7 A boy's cotton shirt. The seams of the raglan sleeves, the collar and belt have been decorated with a simple cross-stitch border worked over canvas which was removed afterwards.

16

ABOVE
8 Two examples of a harsh seam line, softened by the addition of straight and automatic machine embroidery stitch patterns.

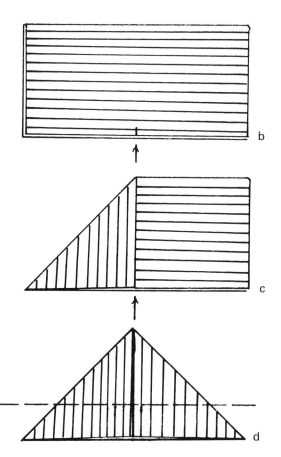

9 How to fold a Somerset point. Horizontal shading indicates the right side of the fabric. The dotted line in (d) represents the stitch line.

10 A wild silk bolero, designed and made by Angela Dewar. Triangular arrangements of Somerset points are inserted into the seams of the patchwork.

facing the right side of the fabric, the triangles pointing away from the seam and the stitch line of the triangle matching up with the stitch line of the dress fabric. (Remember that the triangle has a seam allowance of only 1 cm (½ in.) while the dress may have the usual 1.5 cm (⅝ in.). The stitch line of the triangle must coincide with the stitch line of the dress.) The Somerset points may be placed so that they just touch when the seam is turned right side out or so that they overlap, or some may be placed back to front or behind others. Alternatively, triangles of differing sizes may be grouped together as in figure 10.

Tack the triangles well into place along the stitch line so that they will not move when the

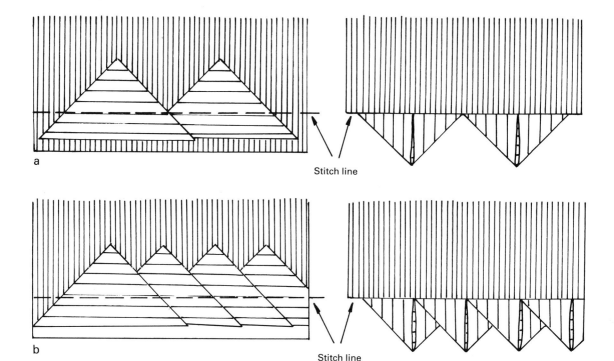

a

Stitch line

b

Stitch line

c

Stitch line

11 How to arrange and sew Somerset points into a seam.

seam is machined or the facing attached in the usual way. The success of Somerset patchwork is largely dependent on the accurate folding of the fabric. Choose materials which will hold a fold easily. Try to avoid a springy synthetic fabric or a very crease-resistant one.

Lacing over a seam

A softening effect can also be obtained by lacing over a seam where two colours meet.

In Pam Monk's design for a culotte suit (*12*) a beige leather thong is laced over a seam where red suede meets brown fabric. The holes in the suede and the fabric are strengthened with metal eyes.

Insertions

Instead of working embroidery over a finished seam, it is possible to make an open decorative join, where the embroidery not only embellishes but also joins the pattern pieces of the garment.

Traditionally insertions are worked on fine fabric, in the seams of lingerie, baby clothes, blouses and summer dresses. Figure 13 shows a Romanian underskirt from the beginning of this century. The raw edges of the fine cotton have been turned under twice and secured with hem stitching. The bottom edge is decorated with a crochet edging and a cross-stitch border in black and red. The side seams are worked in Italian

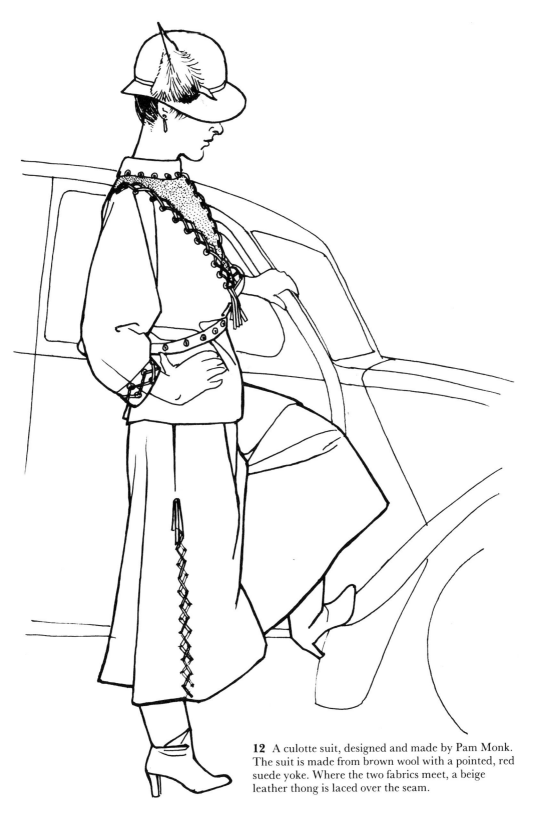

12 A culotte suit, designed and made by Pam Monk. The suit is made from brown wool with a pointed, red suede yoke. Where the two fabrics meet, a beige leather thong is laced over the seam.

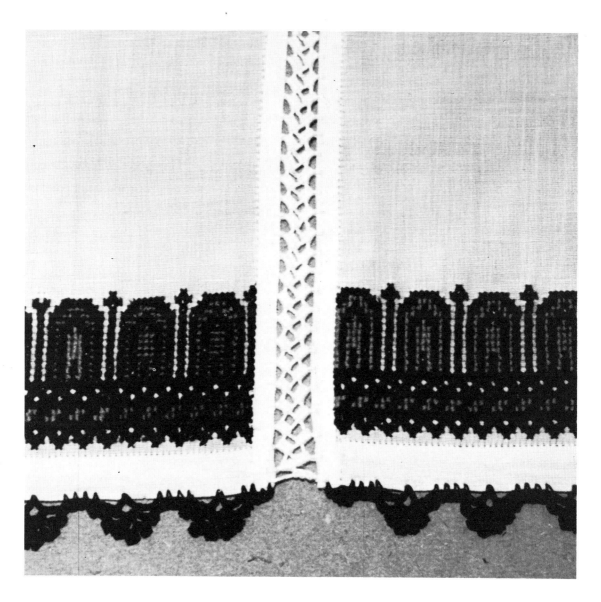

13 A cotton voile underskirt from Roumania, with Italian buttonhole insertion stitches in the side seams. The hem is decorated with a cross-stitch border and crochet edging.

buttonhole insertion using coton à broder. It has been worked into a space of 2 cm (¾ in.).

To prepare pattern pieces for insertion stitches the raw edges must be neatened and strengthened. A simple hem, stitched by machine or hand, will be sufficient for most garments, but not very imaginative. Edges could be bound in a contrasting colour or fabric. They could, for instance, be strengthened with pulled work or hem stitching.

The finished edges of two adjoining pattern pieces are then tacked onto a strong piece of paper of strips of stiff fabric, leaving a gap between them of anything from 0.5 cm (³⁄₁₆ in.) to 3 cm (1¼ in.) wide. Two parallel lines drawn onto the paper or fabric strip, as far apart as the

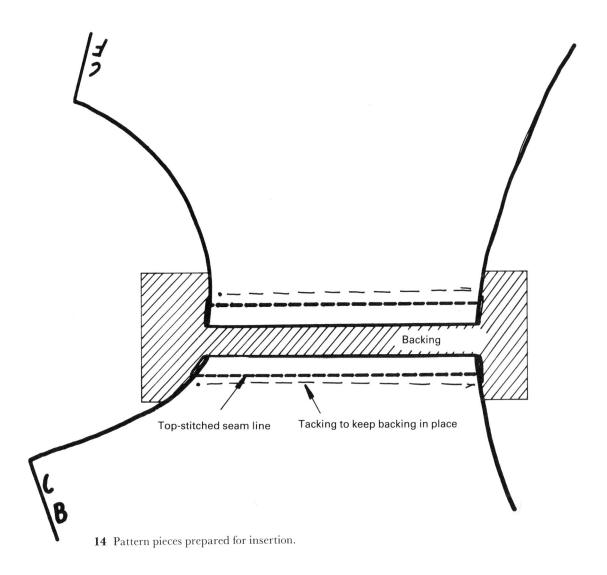

14 Pattern pieces prepared for insertion.

Labels within figure: Backing; Top-stitched seam line; Tacking to keep backing in place

intended width of the insertion, can be used as guidelines and will ensure that the finished seam is even and straight (*14*). The width of an insertion seam varies a great deal with the type of stitch used, the fabric and the thread. It is advisable to work a sampler to determine the right proportions. Threads are usually fastened on and off either on the back of the work or in the fold of the hem. Should it be difficult to secure the thread ends while the work is still attached to the backing, they may be brought through the backing and left there until the stitching is completed and the backing is taken off.

Twisted insertion stitch or faggoting

The hemmed edges of the two pieces of fabric to be joined are tacked onto a backing as usual. The space between the hems varies with fabrics and threads, so it is advisable to work a sampler first, starting with a gap of about 1 cm (⅜ in.). This stitch is easiest worked from left to right:

1 Fasten the working thread in the left corner of the bottom hem and bring it out in the fold of the hem.

2 Take the needle diagonally across and under

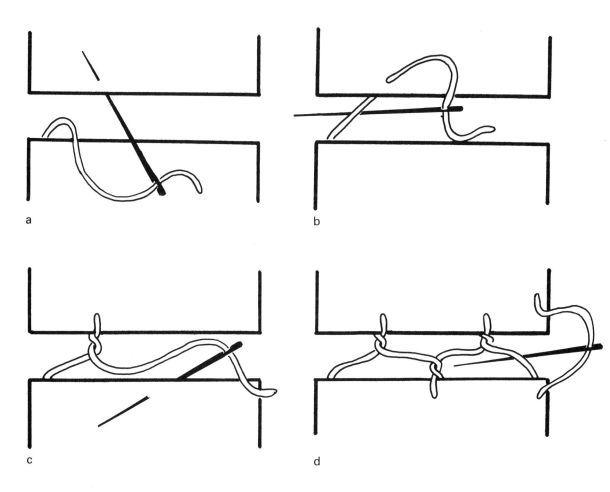

a   b

c   d

15 Twisted insertion stitch or faggoting.

the top hem. Bring the needle from the back of the work to the front, about 3 mm (⅛ in.) above the edge of the hem. Pull the working thread tight.

3 Thread the needle underneath the diagonal bar from right to left.

4 Take the needle diagonally across and underneath the bottom hem. Bring the needle from the back of the work to the front, about 3 mm (⅛ in.) below the edge of the hem. Pull the working thread tight.

5 Thread the needle underneath the near diagonal bar from right to left.

Repeat from step 2 until the seam is finished. Fasten off the working thread, either in the hem or at the back of the work.

For further use of insertion stitches, see page 46.

Italian buttonhole insertion stitch

1 Fasten the working thread to the back of the finished edge on the right-hand side of the insertion seam and bring it through to the front about 3 mm (⅛ in.) from the fold of the edge.

2 Stretch the thread horizontally across the gap to the left-hand side of the seam and insert the needle from the front of the work to the back, about 2 cm (¾ in.) from the edge, through all the layers of fabric in the hem of the finished edge, but not through the backing paper or strips of stiff fabric.

3 Bring the needle and thread to the front again, underneath the horizontal bar. Work about four buttonhole stitches around it, from the left-hand edge to the centre of the bar.

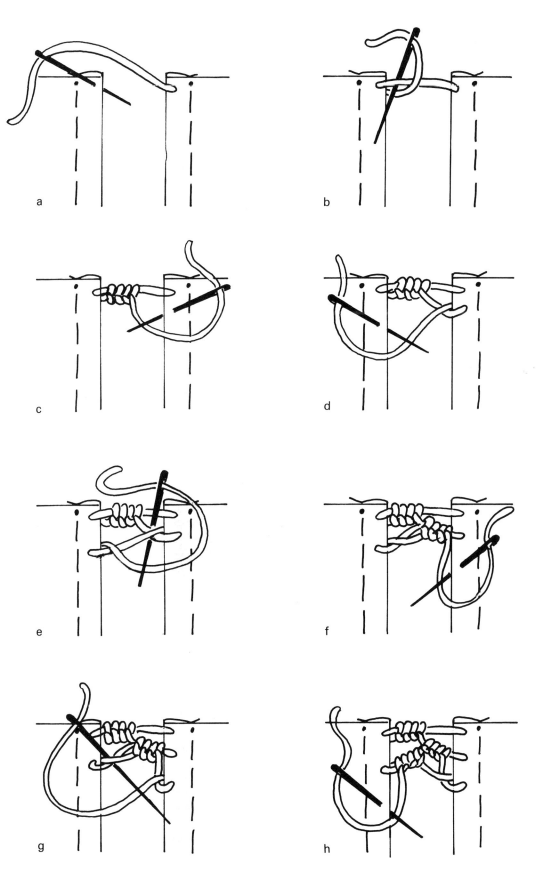

a

b

c

d

e

f

g

h

16 Italian buttonhole insertion stitch.

4 Stretch the working thread across to the right-hand side of the seam, insert the needle from the front to the back, 3 mm (⅛ in.) from the edge and about ½ cm (³⁄₁₆ in.) below the first stitch.

5 Bring the needle to the front of the work above this small bar and take it across to the left-hand side of the seam.

6 Make a similar stitch into the left-hand hem, 3 mm (⅛ in.) from the edge, but 1 cm (⅜ in.) below the previous stitch on this side.

7 Bring the working thread to the front above this new bar and take it to the centre of the seam, to the last one of the four buttonhole stitches.

8 Work four more buttonhole stitches around both threads leading to the second stitch on the right-hand side of the seam.

9 Insert the needle from the front to the back, 2 mm (⅛ in.) from the edge and 1 cm (⅜ in.) below the last stitch.

10 Bring the thread to the front, above the new stitch, and take it to the centre of the seam.

11 Work four buttonhole stitches around both threads leading to the last stitch on the left-hand side of the seam.

12 Insert the needle from the front to the back as before, and repeat from step 8 until the seam is finished or the working thread runs out.

After the final group of buttonhole stitches, bring the working thread to the edge and stitch through to the back of the work as usual, but instead of bringing the thread back to the front, fasten it off in the fold of the hem or the back of the work. A new thread is fastened on the same side of the seam and brought to the front above the last stitch without going through the fabric. The stitching is continued as before.

A beaded insertion
In contrast, figure 17 shows a woollen jacket by Dorothy Regler. The raw edges of the fabric are bound with felt and joined using the following method, with wooden beads adding further interest.

17 Detail of a woollen jacket, designed and made by Dorothy Regler. The seams are bound with pinked felt strips and joined by hand, inserting a wooden bead with each stitch. Hand embroidery stitches have been added on either side of the seam.

Cut strips of felt, 5 cm (2 in.) wide. The felt should be a wide width, to avoid having to make joins. Fold the strips in half and machine along the fold, as close as possible to the edge. The strips are then given their decorated edge, either in a pinking machine, with pinking shears or by cutting with ordinary scissors.

The edges of the jacket should be cut to the fitting line. Place the cut edge of the jacket inside the felt strip and push in as far as possible. With the jacket right-side up work a row of machine stitching along the edge. This attaches the strip to the jacket. Fold the strip over to enclose the jacket edge. Machine on the right side, 1 cm (⅜ in.) from the fold. Add a row of tiny zigzag stitches against the line of straight stitching. Work further decoration by hand, joining the edges with beads, using double strong thread, working backwards and forwards in a zigzag fashion within the felt so that the stitches do not show. This type of seam is best worked horizontally from left to right.

Inserted embroideries
Insertions of a different kind can be made by sewing a length of embroidered fabric, lace, broderie anglaise or crochet of even width and with firm edges between the two fabrics to be

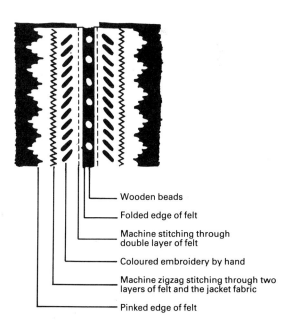

Wooden beads

Folded edge of felt

Machine stitching through double layer of felt

Coloured embroidery by hand

Machine zigzag stitching through two layers of felt and the jacket fabric

Pinked edge of felt

18 Method of joining the seams of the jacket in figure 17.

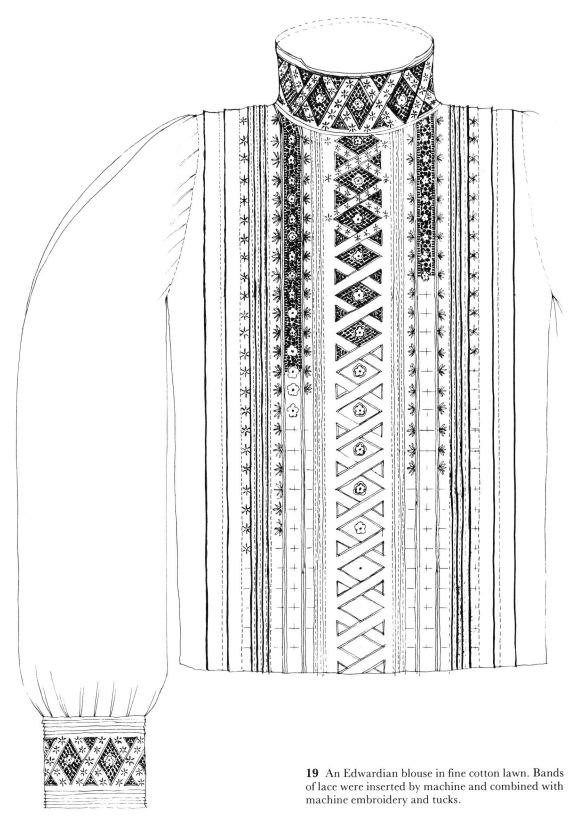

19 An Edwardian blouse in fine cotton lawn. Bands of lace were inserted by machine and combined with machine embroidery and tucks.

joined (*19*). The sewing can be done by machine or hand. As these insertions may be quite wide and are set between the dress pattern pieces, their width will add to the size of the garment. Unless the paper pattern used has already allowed for this, some adjustment will be necessary. Very large insertions or areas with shaped edges are best applied first, and then the surplus fabric cut away from the back. In this case, the edges of the fabric can be neatened beforehand, in the following way.

Mark the sewing line very accurately with a tacking thread. Work a small, close zigzag stitch just beyond the marked line. When the insertion has been applied, the surplus fabric should be trimmed against the line of zig-zag stitching. If the insertion is sewn in with tight buttonhole stitch or machined with satin stitch, further neatening may not be necessary.

Insertion stitches can be used to make up an openwork embroidered fabric from rouleaux, braids, ribbons, tapes or bands. This can then be inserted into the garment.

To make this type of insertion, tack the braids or ribbons onto a stiff backing of paper or fabric. They can be arranged in any design with differing spaces in between, into which the insertion stitches are worked. Rouleaux, braids and tapes which are on the cross and are easily arranged in curves may be tacked down in a pattern previously drawn onto the backing. Unless lace stitches and needleweaving are used as well as insertion stitches, the spaces between the tapes should not exceed 3 cm (1¼ in.), or the resulting fabric will be too flimsy.

3 Borders and edges

Instead of using a seam as a guideline for decoration, any edge of a garment, for example the hem line, the edge of a flounce or the lower edge of a sleeve can be enriched with embroidered borders.

Border designs are usually linear or repeat patterns and may be simple or elaborate. Many embroidery techniques are suitable: patchwork, quilting, appliqué, couching, cross stitch and surface stitchery are only a few.

Linear border patterns

A linear border pattern is easy to design with the help of cut paper. Cut a number of paper strips of varying widths in any colour and arrange them on the dress pattern to be used. Change them around, bring them close together or further apart, overlap them or cross them, until a pleasing effect is achieved; bear in mind the relationship of the border to the garment as a whole. Stick the paper shapes down. Thinner and curved lines can be added with a felt pen (20).

The border may be stitched on the sewing machine, applying braids, ribbons, laces and cords. These may be sewn down with either straight stitches or zigzag stitch. They may also be effectively combined with automatic embroidery stitches or with hand embroidery. Ribbons and lace may be gathered into ruffles or left flat (21).

A linear border need not be confined to the straight edge of a garment. It can be curved to follow the lower front edge of a jacket (22) or bolero, or the edge of a wide sleeve. Where rows of English quilting are used in these areas, interfacing will not be required as the wadding provides adequate body. In Valerie Riley's painted and quilted bolero (23), the quilted lines of the armhole border are in keeping with the overall use of the technique and make a good, crisp finish.

Most modern machines can be fitted with a

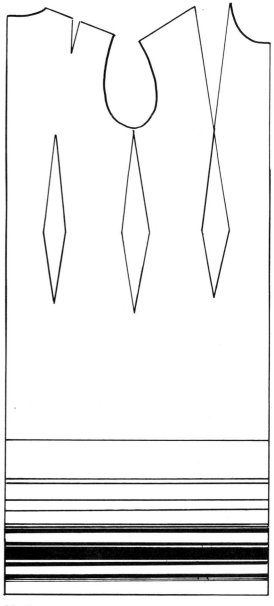

20 Cut paper strips of varying widths arranged on a dress pattern to achieve a balanced relationship between the border and the garment as a whole.

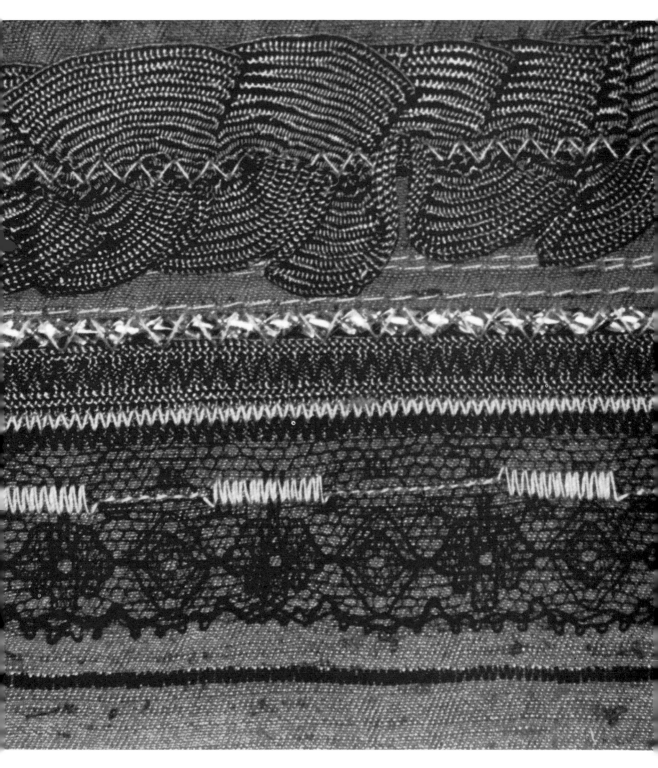

21 A sample of braids, ribbons, lace and cords
applied by machine to make a border.

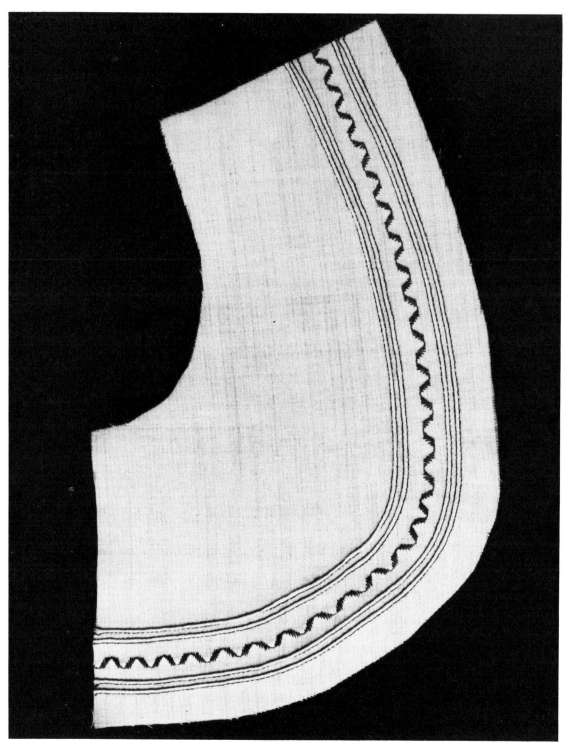

22 A linear border of simple automatic machine
stitching, following a curved edge. The tucks have
been worked with a twin needle.

23 A sunset in the Ashdown Forest inspired Valerie Riley's design for this painted, quilted and embroidered bolero. The landscape has been painted onto the fabric in colours ranging from light orange to deep purple. Trees are suggested by French knots.

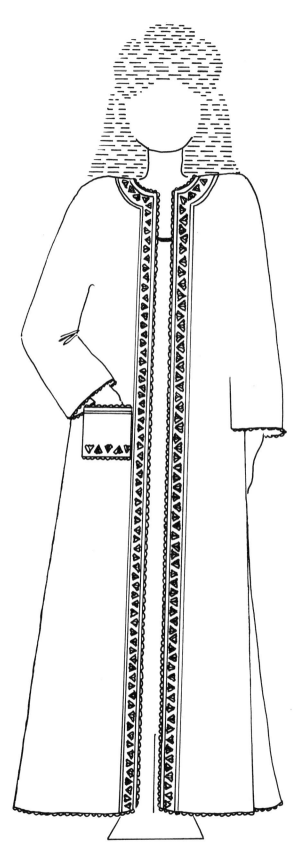

24 A dressing gown with a quilted border. The design for the border was taken from studies of shells.

25 Detail of quilted and tucked border for a dressing gown, with shell motifs. Designed and made by Diana Byers.

twin needle. This can be used to make attractive pin-tucks, which combine well with automatic stitches when used to build up a border. They also have the added advantage of being easier to work than traditional tucking when the fabric is on the bias, such as on the curved hem of a skirt. Pin-tucks made in this way are more successful on lighter weight fabrics. Always check that the chosen fabric behaves as desired by working a trial piece and by experimenting with different threads. To design a border pattern using pin-tucks, adopt the method described for a linear border.

Geometric and figurative designs

Ideas for geometric and figurative design patterns (24, 25) can be found all around, in everyday articles, in nature and architecture or, already two-dimensional, in books, newspapers, photographs, paintings and magazines (26, 27). The same design can be worked in different techniques. The basic lines of the pattern will be the same, but its character will change. For instance, one could quilt a pattern around the hem of a woollen skirt and repeat it in surface stitchery on the edge of the sleeves of a silk blouse made to wear with the skirt. Patterns on clothes can be repeated on accessories such as handbags (28).

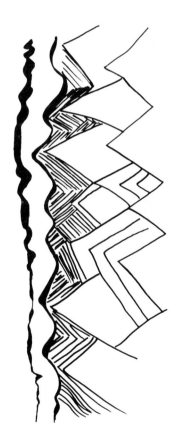

b

a

26 (a) A study of the shell *Oliva porphyria*.
　　(b) An enlargement of part of the shell study.

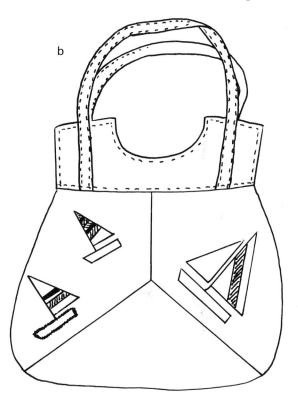

FAR LEFT
27 An interpretation of figure 26(b) into a border design. White satin ribbons were dyed different shades of pink and cut and folded into Somerset points. The points were arranged into two irregular, opposing lines and rows of machine stitching were worked between them.

LEFT AND BELOW
28 Motifs taken from the border of a summer skirt have been repeated on the blouse and beach bag.

Cross stitch over canvas

We are used to seeing a great deal of embroidery on peasant costumes and it is tempting to work, for instance, some of the very attractive cross-stitch borders of central and eastern Europe onto a modern garment. It is possible to work cross stitches and other counted threadwork techniques, such as blackwork, onto finely woven fabrics with the help of needlepoint canvas; use either double canvas; such as Penelope, or single canvas. The canvas is cut roughly to the size of the embroidery and tacked onto the right side of the garment, along the area to be embroidered. The stitches are worked over the threads of the

canvas into the fabric. When the embroidery is completed, the garment is either soaked in hand-warm water, or a towel saturated with warm water is placed on top of the embroidery to soften the canvas. After a few minutes it is possible to withdraw the canvas, thread by thread. First ease out the shorter threads, then the longer ones (29).

Decorated edges

To decorate the very edge of a garment the plain outline can be embellished, either by working hand or machined edgings into the fabric of the garment, or by adding separately worked edgings, such as lace, crochet, fringes or frills.

29 Cross stitch over canvas:
(a) Cross-stitch border, worked over canvas onto cotton fabric (top).
(b) Some of the canvas threads have been withdrawn (bottom).

RIGHT
30 A child's pinafore dress with machine scallop stitch edge on neck, frill and yoke.

Machined edges

Most modern and a number of older domestic sewing machines will work some decorative edges. The automatic scallop stitch makes a

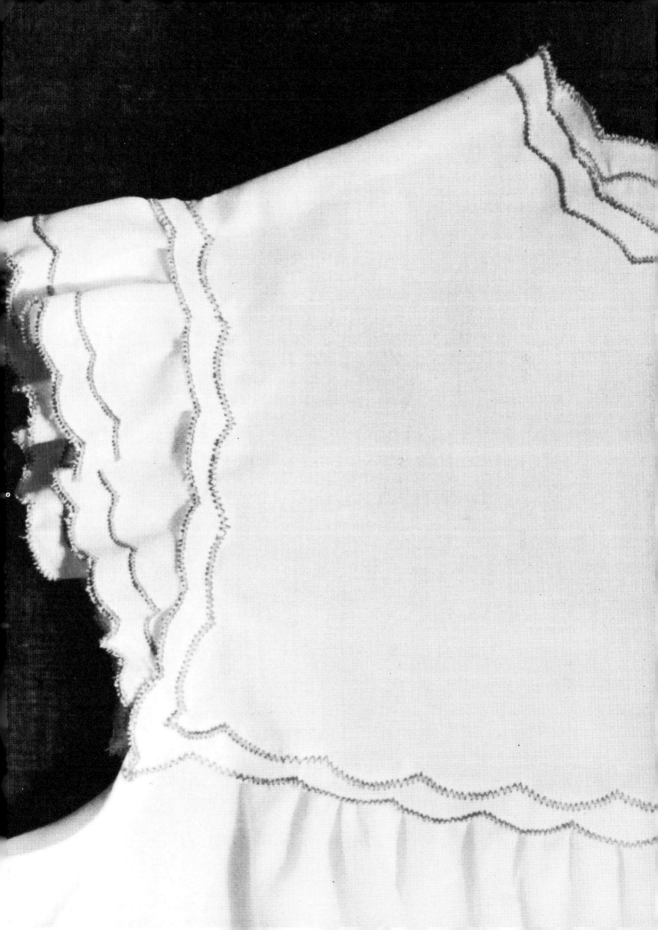

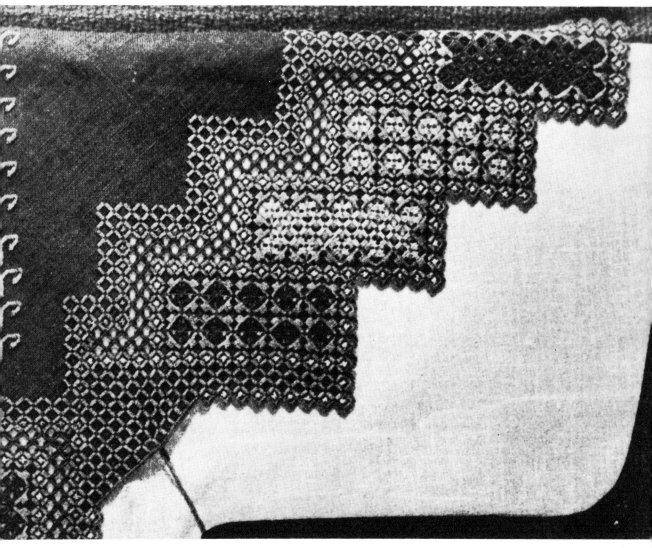

delicate finish for frills or plain edges and is used for necklines, collars, cuffs and hems. Further rows of stitching can be added which will give the fabric more body. It is vital to try out the technique on a piece of the chosen fabric before working on the garment. Too soft a fabric will result in a messy finish and one too thick will not take satin stitch well. Set the machine to a close satin stitch (as for buttonholing) and the automatic scallop stitch. Make adjustments to the settings, if necessary. Fabrics which work well for this type of embroidery include viyella, organdie, firm cottons, lawns and lightweight wools. A pair of very sharp, curved scissors is useful for trimming away the surplus fabric when the stitching has been done.

31 An example of a Hardanger edge from a detachable bodice made by Heide Jenkins. See figure 95, page 100.

An example of this type of edging can be seen in figure 31. This Victorian-style pinafore dress was made simply and quickly, part of the embroidery being incorporated in the construction of the garment. After joining the side seams of the skirt the lower edge and all the edges of the yoke were stitched, along the cutting line, with one row of automatic scallop stitch, and the surplus fabric was cut away. The edges of all the frills were embroidered with two rows of scallops, approximately 1 cm (⅜ in.) apart. The underarm curves on the sides of the skirt were bound with a narrow bias strip of self-fabric. The shoulder seam edges of the seam frills and the top edge of the skirt were then neatened.

After both skirt and frills had been gathered up to the correct size, they were pinned and tacked into position, 1.5 cm (⅝ in.) under the finished edges of the skirt, yoke and shoulders. The second row of scallop stitch was then worked, approximately 1 cm (⅜ in.) away from the edge, thus making a neat, flat attachment in a decorative way.

Another machine-made edge is the shell edge, which is particularly useful for fine fabrics such as chiffon and light silks.

Machine embroidery will follow any curve quite easily, around a neck or armhole edge or the curved hem of circular skirt.

Hand-made edges

Straight edges on garments, such as the hem of a gathered skirt or neck openings, are suitable for hand embroidery. On peasant costume the straight bottom edge of the apron has often been highly decorated. Norwegian costume shows beautiful Hardanger work with deep edges and broad borders.

There is a variety of lacy edges which may be worked by hand. Many of these are based on buttonhole stitch. An example of a simple buttonholed edge can be seen in figure 32, decorating a christening bonnet. A type of buttonhole filling stitch, detached buttonhole, was also used to work the butterflies on the bonnet. A firm, single thread should be used for this type of edge and care must be taken to join in a fresh thread smoothly. The edge is worked in groups of three arches at a time (*33*).

A number of base threads are laid in loops and then covered with buttonhole stitches. The loops are arranged in groups of three, two along the edge of the bonnet and one connecting the two. To enable the embroidery to be worked with some speed and economy of thread, each step has to be considered in advance to allow continuous stitching.

Fasten the working thread into the left-hand corner of the edge or hem which is to be decorated. Lay a loop of suitable size along the edge, towards the right, anchoring it with a small stitch through the fabric. To make sure that the loops are of an even size, the base threads may be laid around a finger, pencil or rolled-up paper.

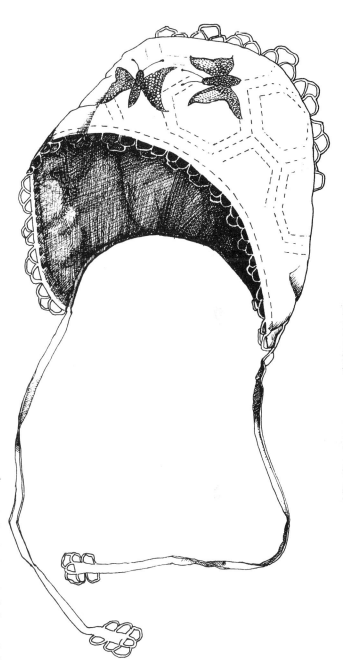

32 A christening bonnet of cotton lawn with a hand-sewn ringed buttonhole edging. The bonnet is hand-quilted and decorated with butterflies worked in hollie point (a form of detached buttonhole stitch).

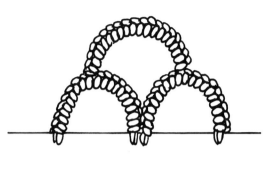
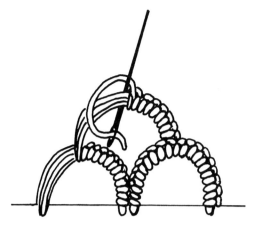
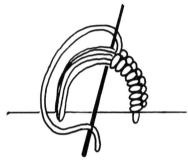
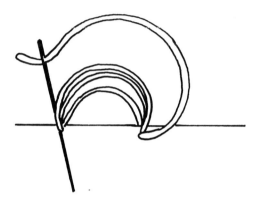

Reinforce this loop three more times, by going back to the beginning, then forward, stitching through the same hole as before, and back again to the beginning. The loop now consists of four base threads. Cover these threads tightly with buttonhole stitches, starting from the left. Finish by taking the thread once through the fabric, near the right-hand anchor point of the loop.

Lay four base threads for the next loop along the edge of the fabric, cover them with buttonhole stitches, as before, working from left to right, but only as far as the apex of the loop. Lay three base threads only for the third loop, reaching from the apex of the second loop back to the apex of the first loop.

Cover the base threads of the third loop with buttonhole stitches, as before, working from left to right. When the centre of the second loop is reached, continue buttonholing to finish the second half of the second loop.

Anchor the working thread by taking it once through the fabric. Work any following groups of buttonholed loops in the same fashion.

The buttonhole stitches should be worked tight enough to cover the base threads completely, but not so tight that they cause distortion and puckering.

Another hand embroidery technique which can be used on edges is pulled work. Although these edges are traditionally worked on the counted thread of linen it is possible to work them evenly on a voile without counting each thread, thereby widening the scope of this type of treatment. This work also looks very effective on an evenweave woollen fabric such as nun's veiling, or on a coarser wool such as a hopsack or fine tweed (*34*). For pulled work the embroidery thread should generally be of the same thickness as the yarn of the fabric.

Edgings can be elaborated into borders so that they become the most prominent design feature. Two examples of this can be seen in figures 36

34 A woollen shawl with a drawn thread border, a pulled work edge of four-sided stitch and a deep fringe. Designed and made by Sonja Moore.

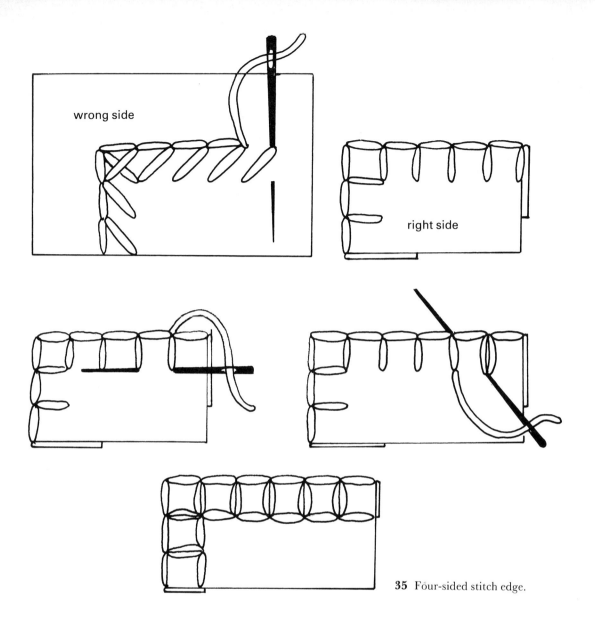

wrong side

right side

35 Four-sided stitch edge.

and 37. Both designs are based on a similar idea, although figure 36 is much more elaborate than figure 37. For the neck edge of a summer dress, worked in a dull, silky polyester, Jennifer Stuart designed a pattern to be worked with rouleaux and faggoting stitch. For details on how to construct this type of work, see page 27 (inserted embroideries).

To make up lengths of rouleaux (*38*), cut a strip of bias fabric. Fold it in half lengthwise, with right sides together. Stitch, leaving the ends open. Leave the seam allowance untrimmed as it will act as a filler for the tube of fabric. Attach a length of strong thread to one end of the tube at the seam. Pull the thread gently through the

tubing, using a large needle or bodkin. Insert the eye first. There are rouleaux turners available which are made from a long wire, with a latched hook at one end, but these would not be suitable for extremely long pieces of rouleaux. If a firmer rouleau is required the method is slightly different and a cord is used. Cut a bias strip, wide enough to cover the chosen thickness of cord plus the seam allowance. Cut a piece of cord twice the length of the bias. Sew an end of the bias strip to the centre of the cord. Fold the right side of the fabric over the cord and stitch, using a cording foot. Trim the seam turning and pull the enclosed cord out of the tubing.

Fine corded rouleaux should be used to make

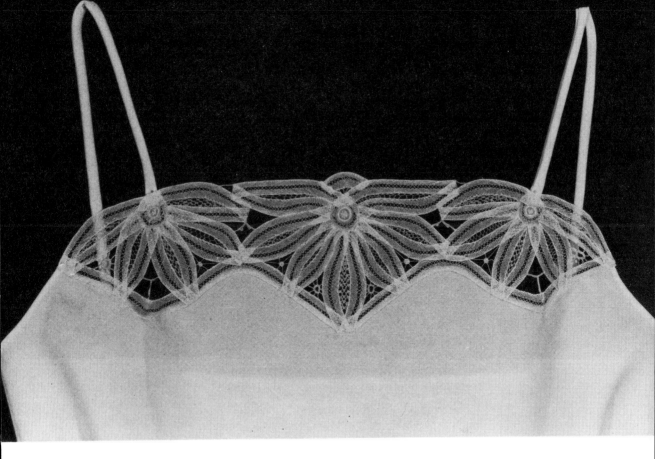

36 A camisole with tape lace edging, designed and made by Mary Anderson.

the row of button loops which are often used on the back of a wedding dress and these loops can also form an attractive edge decoration for necklines or at the lower edge of sleeves.

Figure 36 shows a camisole made by Mary Anderson. The upper edge of the bodice front is decorated with a wide, shaped band of delicate tape lace. This type of tape or point lace originated in the seventeenth century and it was intended to imitate elaborate Venetian needlepoint laces.

The lace is constructed from bobbin-tape (see Suppliers', page 142). The tape is shaped and joined and the shapes filled with decorative needlepoint stitches, buttonhole rings or *couronnes*, and spider webs. Bobbin tape is available in white or cream and may be plain or

patterned in weave. There are several widths, ranging from 3 mm (⅛ in.) to 8 mm (⅜ in.). For the needlepoint filling stitches, a fine twist thread should be used. Before undertaking a large project in tape lace, a beginner should first try a small sample. The materials required to make a small piece of lace are:

> 2 or 3 metres (6 or 10 ft) of tape
> One reel of matching sewing thread
> Tacking thread in a contrasting colour
> Crewel needle
> Ballpoint needle
> A piece of stiff brown paper at least twice the size of the design to be worked

1 Fold the brown paper in half, for added strength, and tack it together.

2 Transfer the design onto the brown paper.

3 Lay the tape over the design, right side down, and tack it through the paper, along the centre,

37 Neck edge of a summer dress, designed and made by Jennifer Stuart. Tape lace techniques have been used but the tape was replaced with rouleaux made from the dress fabric.

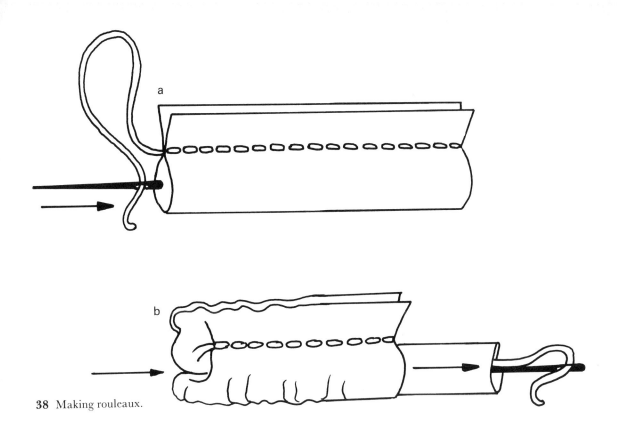

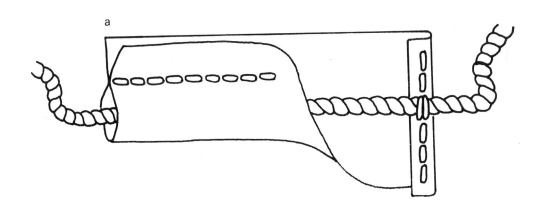

38 Making rouleaux.

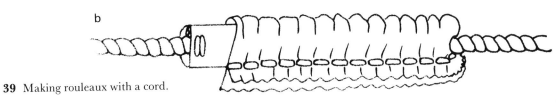

39 Making rouleaux with a cord.

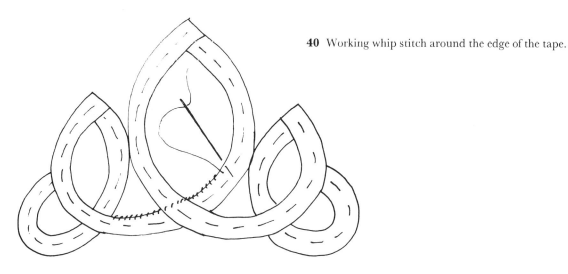

40 Working whip stitch around the edge of the tape.

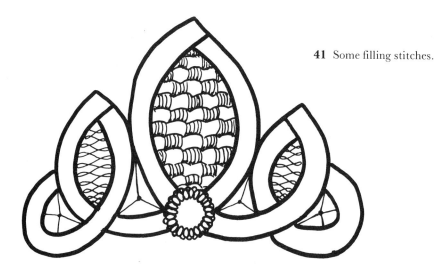

41 Some filling stitches.

with small stitches. Ease the tape around curves, keeping the outer edges flat.

4 Using the crewel needle and the matching thread, work a whip stitch around the edges of the tape (*40*). Stitch approximately 2.5 cm (1 in.) at a time and gently draw up the curved edges, to shrink away fullness. Whip all around the design, stitching together all crossings and joins.

5 Using the ballpoint needle, work the filling

stitches (*41*). Begin the first stitch with a very small knot and overcast once.

6 When all the filling stitches have been completed, turn the paper over and remove all the tacking stitches. Buttonhole rings or French knots may be added to the right side of the work at this stage (*42*).

Two stitches which are commonly used as filling stitches for tape lace are fagotting (see page 23) and pea stitch. Stitches which give a raised texture are buttonhole ring and French knots.

1· A jacket for a child, designed
and made by Sue Tomkins.
The background fabric of blue
wool is embroidered with crewel
work stitches, including fishbone
stitch, long and short stitch,
Cretan stitch, stem stitch and a
variety of laid filling stitches.
The design has been arranged to
fit well into the shape of the jacket,
on both the front and back, and
the jungle scene continues around
the whole body of the garment
without a break in the pattern.

2 A sun dress, designed and made by Mary Holland. The wide shoulder straps are decorated with rows of herringbone stitches in differing sizes and textural contrast is provided by groups of eyelet holes.

3 A patchwork waistcoat designed and made by Angela Dewar. Liberty Tana lawn and plain silks are combined in a simple geometric pattern which was both pieced and quilted by machine.

To make a buttonhole ring (*42*):

1 Make a foundation ring by winding the embroidery thread around a stiletto or knitting needle of the required size.

2 Working with the same length of thread, buttonhole closely around the ring, joining the first and last stitches. Leave the thread attached and use it to sew the ring onto the lace.

Be certain to allow enough thread in the needle to complete the ring, leaving some spare with which to sew it to the lace. After practice, the correct amount will become obvious.

Tape lace may be applied onto or inserted into clothes, using a close zig-zag machine stitch.

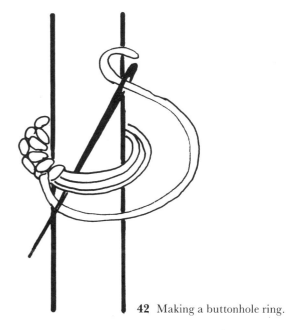

42 Making a buttonhole ring.

4 Collars and neck decorations

A collar encircles the neckline of a garment. It sits in a most prominent position, between the wearer's face and the dress, and it should try to flatter both. It may be an integral part of a garment or completely separate and only tacked or buttoned into place. A detachable collar will allow more freedom in the choice of decoration, as it can be cleaned separately from the dress.

All styles of collar are suitable for embroidery. As with all designing, it is important to consider carefully the shape of the area which is to be decorated, and to develop a design for that shape.

Hand cutwork

Simple cutwork by hand is a method which is suitable for a small area, such as a collar. It can have a very open, lacey effect or can contain more areas of plain fabric. The outlines of the design are worked in buttonhole stitch. The background fabric is cut away, but the design motifs remain and this must be the main consideration when working out a design. The pattern must be drawn so that the cutwork will not fall apart when the background fabric is cut away from the buttonhole stitching, nor must any parts of it hang loosely, where they will curl up and look untidy. A good way of checking that all is well is to black out or cut away on the paper patterns the parts which are to be removed (43). Any loose parts of the design will soon become apparent, and corrections can be made (44). On the simple cutwork collar in figure 45 the fuchsia blossoms were designed to 'grow' out of the collar points.

To make cutwork by hand, first outline the design with small running stitches (44). This will help to pad the stitching slightly. Work buttonhole stitch closely over the running stitches. Always keep the knots of the buttonhole stitch against the edges of that part of the design which is to be cut away. When all the buttonhole stitching is complete, cut away the background parts of the design. Use a twisted thread rather

than a stranded thread for this embroidery, such as silk, coton à broder or coton perlé.

Machine cutwork

Cutwork can also be worked on the sewing machine. Figure 46 shows a collar made by Frances Gibb, using an old treddle machine. The collar was worked on white organdie, using a machine embroidery thread of mercerised cotton (no. 50).

Several designs were considered before the final arrangement of motifs was chosen (47). It is important to spend some time 'playing' with designs in this way and to explore several possibilities before making the final decision. This collar was worked by an expert, but it is quite possible, with some practice, to become proficient enough to work some simple cutwork patterns using the sewing machine. Figure 48 shows a few varied motifs worked on organdie. Organdie is a good fabric for machine cutwork, as it is firm but has a delicate appearance.

To work cutwork by machine, first mark the design onto the fabric. A water-soluble pen is suitable for transferring designs onto organdie for machine cutwork. As the organdie is transparent, place it over the drawn design and make a tracing directly onto the fabric. Fix the organdie very tightly into a tambour frame. The tambour frame should be placed under the needle with the fabric lying flat, against the flat bed of the machine. On a free-arm machine, use the detachable sewing table provided. This allows a steadier movement of the frame while sewing.

Lower the feed-dog of the machine or cover the teeth with the plate provided. Remove the presser foot, but remember that the pressure lever must *always* be lowered while sewing, otherwise the tension will not be correct and the thread will gather up into a tangle on the underside.

Outline the shape which is to be cut away once or twice with straight stitching. If rows of

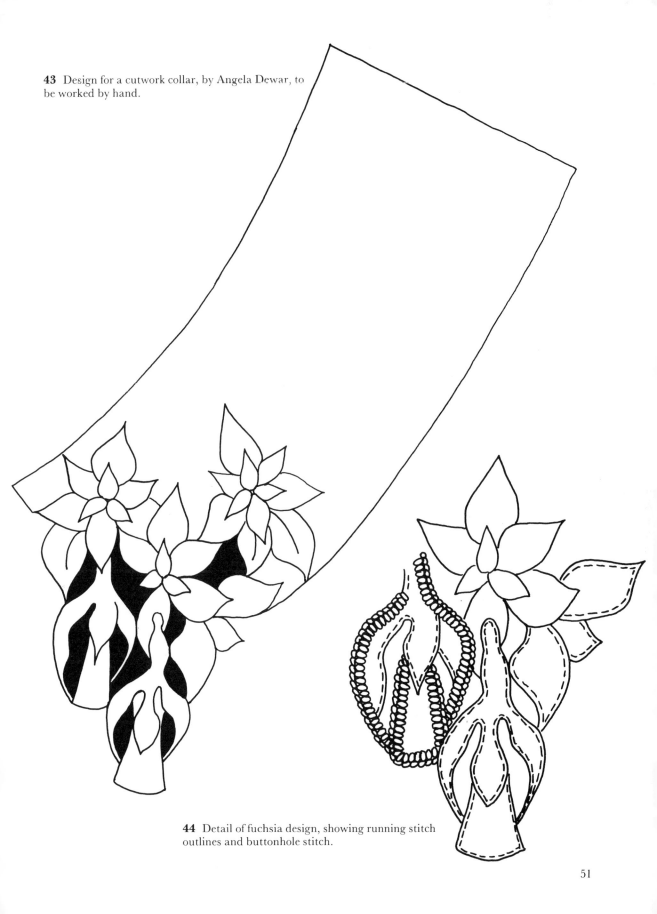

43 Design for a cutwork collar, by Angela Dewar, to be worked by hand.

44 Detail of fuchsia design, showing running stitch outlines and buttonhole stitch.

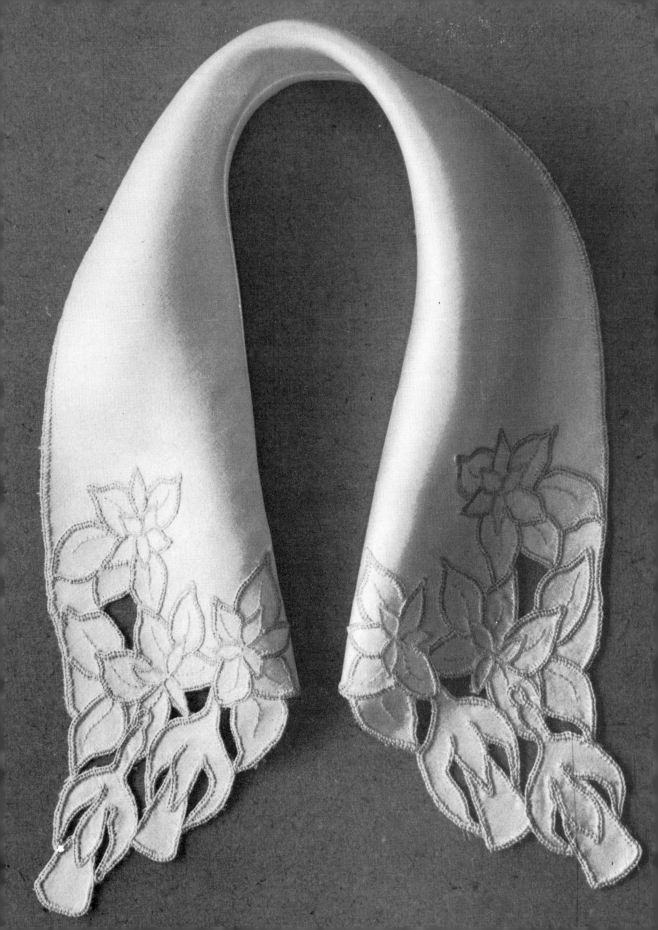

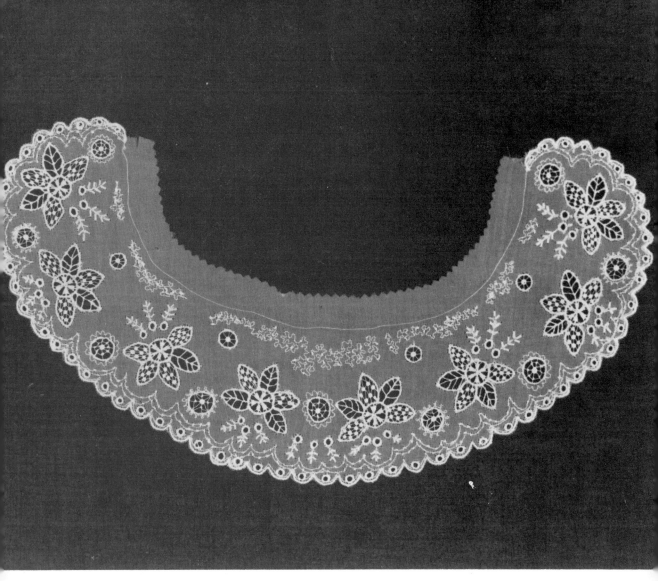

LEFT
45 Angela Dewar's cutwork collar with fuchsia
blossoms. The embroidery was worked in silk thread
on a silk satin fabric.

ABOVE
46 A collar, designed and made by Frances Gibb,
using an old treddle sewing machine. The white
organdie was embroidered with machine embroidery
thread, no. 50.

touching motifs are being worked in (as in figure
49) the shapes should be worked alternately,
completing each cut section before moving on to
the next. If this order of working is not observed,
the cutwork may fall apart. After the outline has
been stitched, the fabric is cut away, using sharp-
pointed and curved scissors. The work will
probably have to be removed from the machine
for this job. Resume the stitching, beginning with
an open zig-zag stitch once more around the
outline, and then working to and fro across the
open shape with straight stitch, creating formal
or informal patterns within the space. To start
and finish the stitching securely, allow the needle
to stitch on one spot for a few stitches. The
technique requires practice and some trial
samples should be worked before beginning the
chosen project.

47 Preliminary studies by Frances Gibb for her organdie collar.

48 Samples of simple machine embroidery cutwork on organdie, made by a first year City and Guilds student.

49 Working order for machine cutwork with touching motifs. The open shapes should be worked alternately, completing each cut section before moving on to the next. If this order of work is not observed, the embroidery may fall apart.

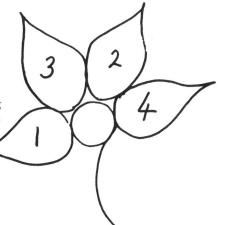

Needle lace

A splendid example of hand sewing can be seen in figures 50 and 51. This collar, by Meriel Tilling, is made of a fine, white voile embroidered in a variety of pulled work stitches with some shadow work included. This type of needle lace was extremely popular during the eighteenth century, when it was known as Dresden work or Pointe de Saxe and modern examples of such a fine technique are not often seen. It is also closely related to the Ayrshire work found on many precious old christening robes. For the embroiderer with skill, patience and good eyesight, this work is extremely satisfying and rewarding.

Quilting

A complete contrast is the shawl collar of the dressing gown shown in figure 52. It has been quilted by machine and, in this case, the garment was completely finished before the embroidery was worked. This is not the usual way to quilt on clothing, but, as the fabric itself was used as the design source, it was the simplest method to use. The motif of the printed fabric has been quilted onto the plain satin facing, working from the underside of the finished collar. When sewing on the back of the work in this way, always check that the machine is producing a good tension on the underside, as well as on the upper surface. The layers of fabric will require careful tacking together.

Normally, quilting should be done before the garment is cut out, since a certain amount of fabric will be taken up as the work progresses. An outline of the pattern piece to be quilted should be tacked onto the fabric.

English quilting (machine method)

1 Press the top and backing fabrics.

2 Mark the design onto the top fabric. (See page 14.)

3 Tack together the top, filling and bottom fabrics. Tack from the centre outwards for small pieces of work, and in a square grid pattern for larger areas.

4 Thread up the machine with the chosen thread. (See page 10.)

5 Select a medium stitch. It is advisable to work a small trial sample. For intricate parts of the design, a small stitch may be necessary.

6 Stitch the design, leaving at least 7 cm (3 in.) of thread at the start and finish of each piece of stitching.

7 When all the stitching is complete, draw the ends through to the back of the work, tie and stitch them securely into the backing fabric.

There is an alternative method of working which is quicker than the first, as it is not necessary to mark the design onto the fabric. It is suitable for small areas, such as waistcoats, collars, cuffs and pockets, or for quilting on leather and suedes (53).

1 Draw the design onto greaseproof paper, using a fine felt-tip pen. Do not use a pencil as this can easily be transferred to the thread during stitching, making it dirty. Remember to keep a copy of the design for reference.

2 Press the top fabric carefully. Once the quilting is complete it is impossible to remove bad creases from the surfaces.

3 Press the backing fabric.

4 Arrange the top, filling and backing fabrics in layers. Smooth them out.

5 Tack all three layers together, working from the centre outwards for small pieces of work and in a square grid pattern for larger areas.

6 Pin or tack the traced design onto the area to be quilted. Needles are more suitable than pins for this, as they do not mark the fabric. If tacking, use a silk thread or a very soft cotton. The design must be attached so that it will not move during stitching.

7 Thread up the machine with the chosen thread. (See page 10.) Select a medium or long stitch. It is advisable to work a trial sample. For intricate corners or curves, a smaller stitch size may be more suitable.

ABOVE RIGHT
50 A collar, designed and made by Meriel Tilling. It is worked in a fine, white voile, embroidered in a variety of pulled work stitches, with some shadow work and buttonhole edging.

RIGHT
51 Detail of Meriel Tilling's collar, showing pulled work stitches, including variations on single faggot stitch, chained border or cable stitch, wave stitch, cross stitch, step stitch, four-sided stitch and honeycomb stitch.

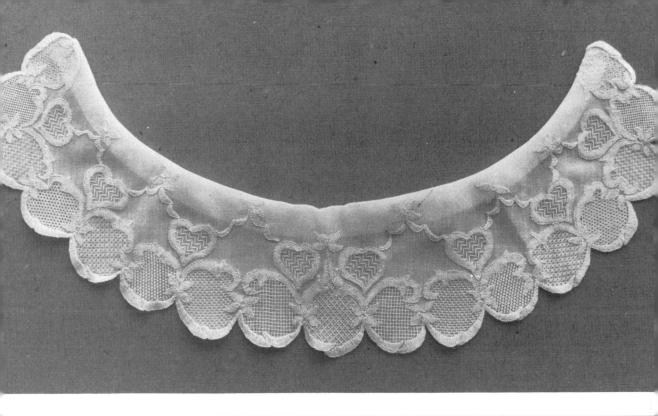

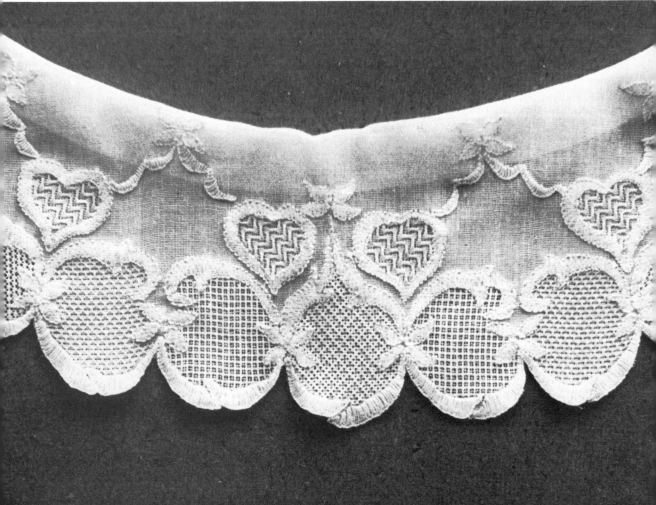

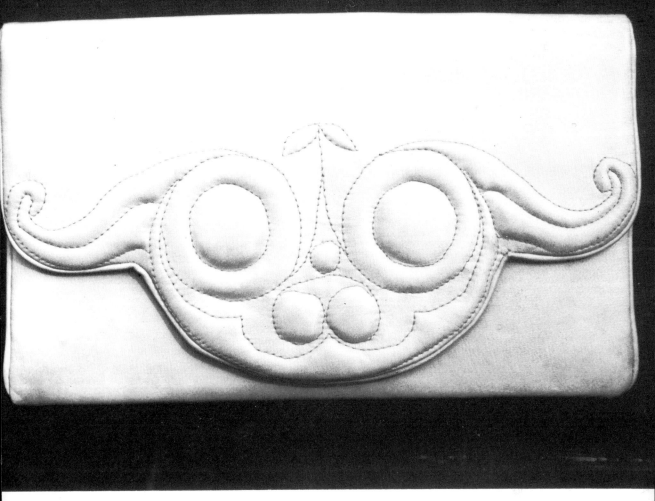

8 Stitch over the design completely. Leave thread ends of at least 7 cm (3 in.) at the beginning and the end of each piece of stitching. This will facilitate secure fastening off.

9 When the design is complete, draw all threads through to the back of the work; tie and sew them firmly into the backing fabric.

10 Gently tear away the tracing paper. Run the tip of a needle along the stitching if the paper is difficult to remove. Use a pair of tweezers to extract any small particles of paper trapped under stitches.

English quilting (hand method)

1 Press the top and the backing fabric.

2 Mark the design onto the top fabric (See page 14.)

3 Arrange the top fabric, filling and backing fabric and smooth them out neatly.

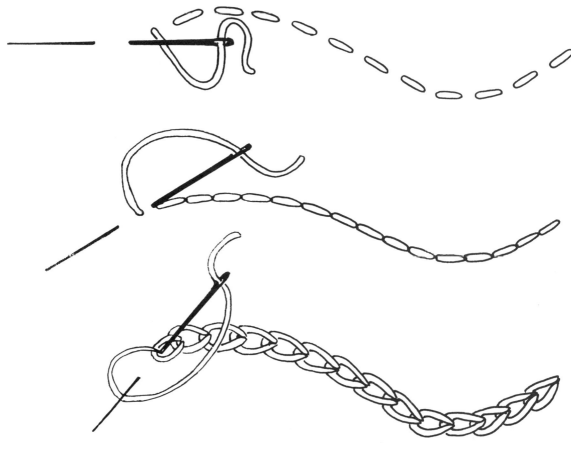

54 Traditional quilting stitches.

4 Tack all three layers together, working from the centre outwards for small pieces and in a square grid for larger areas.

5 If necessary, fix the work onto a slate frame at this stage. Many small pieces may be easily worked without a frame. (See page 12.)

6 Stitch the design. Some stitches traditionally used for hand quilting are: running stitch, back stitch and chain stitch.

Hand and machine quilting can both be enriched by the addition of other surface stitches, such as French knots or Cretan stitch, or beads and spangles, if appropriate.

Dorset crosswheel buttons

Figure 55 shows a neck decoration of a completely different kind. It can be used either as a detachable collar for a dress, or as a necklace,

worn with a low decolletage or strapless dress. The use of Dorset wheel buttons for this unusual collar was suggested to the maker, Mary Holland, on a visit to the local museum at Shaftesbury, in Dorset. The making of Dorset buttons was a cottage industry which died out in the 1850s after the invention of the button-making machine. Of all the types of buttons which were made, the crosswheel type is the only one still used. These buttons are often found on original smocks worn by agricultural workers. The buttons can have a heavy or delicate appearance, depending on the size of the ring and the type of thread used.

For the collar, a number of buttons were made

RIGHT
55 Dorset buttons inspired Mary Holland to make this unusual neck decoration.

56 A modern smock, made by Jane Smith, with Victorian Dorset wheel buttons.

in different sizes, using a mixture of shiny and dull threads. Some were filled in completely and some were left with the spokes showing. The idea for the collar came from arranging the buttons in various ways. At first a symmetrical arrangement was tried but this looked very formal and did not lend itself to the use of the varied buttons. After a good collection of shapes had been made, they were moved about on a piece of net pinned into position, to form an asymmetrical design.

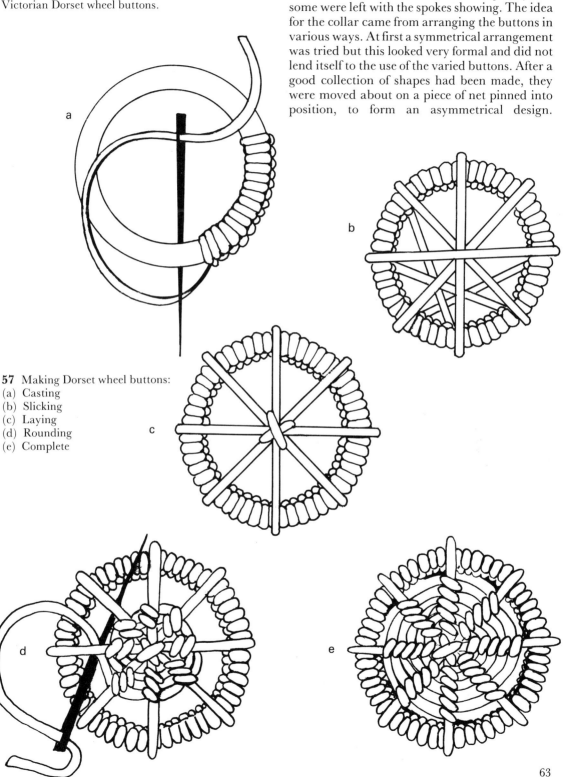

57 Making Dorset wheel buttons:
(a) Casting
(b) Slicking
(c) Laying
(d) Rounding
(e) Complete

However, the finished collar is not exactly the same as the original pinned design because, as the buttons were sewn together, a slight movement occurred at the points where they touched. After the addition of each button, the collar had to be checked to see that it still lay flat. Where the buttons were joined together, a small amount of PVA adhesive was applied to the back of the work, to prevent the joining stitch from working loose. Finally, a hand-made cord (see page 77) was sewn to the neckline of the collar.

Method for buttons

Work a close buttonhole stitch (see page 63) all round the edge of a curtain ring, or similar. This is known as *casting*. Next, push the ridge of knots to the inside of the ring (*slicking*). Working across the ring, lay an even number of spokes, approximately 12. Keep an even tension. This is called *laying*. Form the hub of the wheel with some cross stitches, to separate and tighten the spokes. The final stage of making the button is called *rounding* and consists of working a continual back stitch around the spokes, until the wheel is full (*57*).

5 Yokes

A yoke is a design feature which is used when a basic dress block is divided. In the bodice block this usually happens across the shoulders and upper chest area. In a trouser or skirt block it is usually the area between the waist and hip line. A yoke is often joined to a gathered or bias-cut section of fabric. It is usually a relatively small area and this makes it suitable for some of the finer embroidery techniques. On a bodice the yoke can be made into an important or even dramatic area of decoration. A yoke may be a variety of different sizes and shapes: square, round, scalloped or pointed.

Seminole patchwork

A quick and very effective yoke can be made from a piece of Seminole patchwork worked on the sewing machine. The patchwork is made up and treated as a piece of ordinary material. One of the fabrics used for the patchwork on the child's cotton frock in figure 58 was also used for the skirt of the dress, giving a unity of colour to the whole garment.

At the beginning of this century, the Seminole and Miccosukee Indians of southern Florida started to decorate their clothes with colourful bands of patchwork, known as Seminole patchwork. They used the sewing machine to join narrow strips of fabric in contrasting colour into wider bands. These bands were then cut across the seams into small, multicoloured strips. These were then re-arranged and sewn together into a variety of geometric pattern bands, which were applied or inserted into clothing. Seminole patchwork makes very attractive yokes, cuffs, insertions and edgings.

58 A child's summer dress in cotton with a Seminole patchwork yoke. Designed and made by Gisela Banbury and Angela Dewar.

59 Detail of child's dress.

The patterns look very intricate, but in reality are quite straightforward and quick to make up. Originally, the scale of Seminole patchwork was very small but it translates well to a larger scale. A beginner, inexperienced in handling small patches of fabric, will find it best to work a larger sample first. The child's dress in figure 58 and the instructions and diagram in figures 60-62 show the patchwork made on a similar scale to that worked by the Indians. For a larger sample, cut all strips twice the width given for the dress but still take only 0.5 cm (⅛ in.) seam allowance, to practise the narrow seaming. Choose a closely woven cotton of dress weight. If the fabric will tear easily into narrow strips, without stretching and fraying, this will save time. Otherwise the strips will have to be cut carefully, following the grain of the fabric. The yoke of the dress has been made up of three bands of Seminole patchwork, joined with strips of fabric.

The first band, closest to the skirt, is made up from five strips of fabric in four colours, the two outside colours being the same.

First pattern band

1 Cut two strips in colour A, 4 cm (1½ in.) wide. Cut one strip in colour B, 2 cm (¾ in.) wide. Cut one strip in colour C, 2 cm (¾ in.) wide. Cut one strip in colour D, 1.5 cm (⅝ in.) wide. All strips should be between 50 cm (19½ in.) and 60 cm (23½ in.) long.

2 Taking only 5 mm (³⁄₁₆ in.) seam allowance, sew strip A to B, C and D and add the second strip of A to D.

3 Open the seams or fold them over, according to the space available, and press.

4 Cut this band into 2 cm (¾ in.) wide strips, at right angles to the seams.

5 Re-arrange the strips, as shown in figure 60; pin and sew them together, again taking only 5 mm (³⁄₁₆ in.) seam allowance.

6 Open out all seam allowances and press.

7 Trim the top and bottom edges of the patchwork into straight edges and make sure that they are parallel.

Middle pattern band

1 Cut five strips, in four colours, each 40 cm (16 in.) long:
Cut two strips in colour A, 2 cm (¾ in.) wide. Cut one strip in colour B, 2 cm (¾ in.) wide. Cut one strip in colour C, 2.5 cm (1 in.) wide. Cut one strip in colour D, 3.5 cm (1⅜ in.) wide.

2 Join fabric A to B and C, then add the second strip of fabric A; sew on fabric D as the final strip.

3 Open the seams and press.

4 Cut this band into 2.5 cm (1 in.) wide strips, at right angles to the seams.

5 Cut 2 cm (¾ in.) wide strips from fabric B of the same length as the multicoloured strips, and machine these to the right-hand side of each strip.

6 Pin and sew the strips together in the staggered fashion shown in figure 61 so that each multicoloured strip is separated from the next by a plain strip of fabric.

7 To straighten the ends of a band formed of

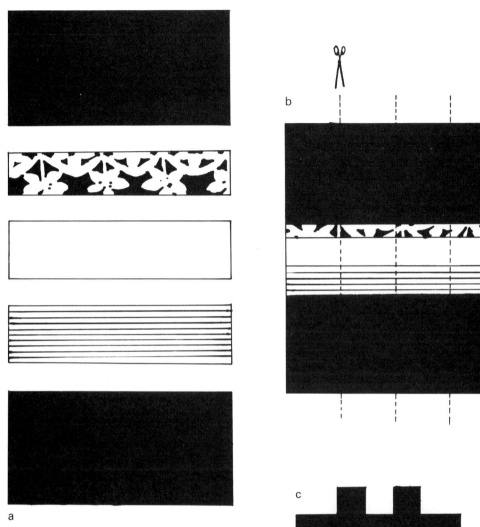

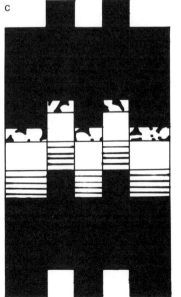

60 The construction of Seminole patchwork, as used in the dress in figure 58. First pattern.

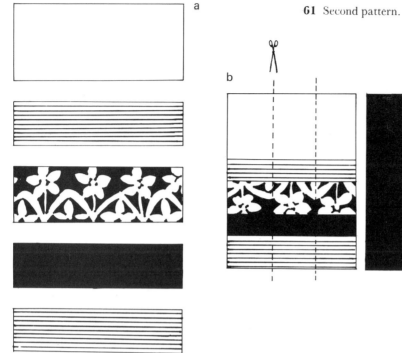

a

61 Second pattern.

b

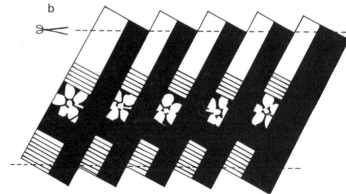

b

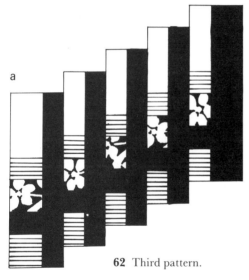

a

62 Third pattern.

diagonal strips, cut the band vertically at any place and change over the two halves, rejoining the two slanting ends in the same pattern as before.

8 Trim the top and bottom of the patchwork band to a straight edge and make sure that they are parallel.

In the band at the top of the yoke in figure 62 only three colours were used, but colour A was used three times.

Top pattern band

1 Cut strips as follows. These strips need only be 25 cm (10 in.) long:

Cut two strips in colour A, 4 cm (1½ in.) wide.
Cut one strip in colour B, 2 cm (¾ in.) wide.
Cut one strip in colour A, 2.5 cm (1 in.) wide.
Cut one strip in colour C, 2.5 cm (1 in.) wide.

2 Join one of the 4 cm (1½ in.) wide strips of colour A to colour B and add the 2.5 cm (1 in.) wide strip of colour A. Now add colour C and the last strip of colour A.

3 Open the seams and press.

4 For this pattern, the band is not cut into strips at right angles to the seams, but at an angle of 45°, as shown in figure 62.

5 Stagger the strips, pin and sew them together, then press open the seams.

6 Trim the top and bottom of the patchwork band to a straight edge, making sure that the edges are parallel. As this pattern is cut on the bias of the fabric, it is very flexible and easily pulled out of shape.

A row of stay stitching along the top and bottom edges will help to keep them straight.

63 Design by Angela Dewar for a silk evening coat with a V-shaped Seminole patchwork yoke, to be worked in a mixture of Liberty lawns and silks.

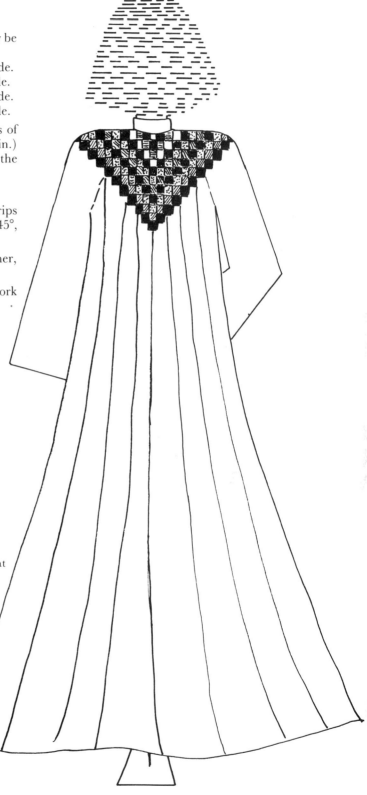

64 Detail of a cotton summer dress, designed and made by Mary Holland. The yoke is decorated with a simple border pattern, made up of couched cord and ric-rac braids in a variety of colours. The same border is repeated around the hem.

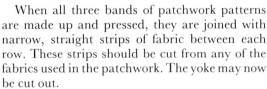

When all three bands of patchwork patterns are made up and pressed, they are joined with narrow, straight strips of fabric between each row. These strips should be cut from any of the fabrics used in the patchwork. The yoke may now be cut out.

Instead of joining four or five narrow strips of different fabrics together to make up the multi-coloured band, a striped fabric may be used. Even if only two or three strips of a fabric are suitable and the rest has to be added, the bulk of the turnings on the back of the work will be considerably reduced. Seminole patchwork has raw edges on the reverse side, so it should be either applied onto another fabric or lined, to make it more tidy and durable.

Seminole patchwork can also be arranged to form a deep, V-shaped yoke (63). To make this, the Seminole strips must be staggered in opposite directions from the centre point. When joining the strips to construct the yoke, stitch within 1 cm (3/8 in.) of the lower edge. Fasten off each seam securely. Press under the 1 cm (3/8 in.) seam allowance along the entire staggered edge. Slip stitch or top stitch by machine to the lower part of the garment.

Other techniques

Many of the methods already described are suitable for decorating yokes. Pin-tucks, applied laces and ribbons and hand-worked border designs fit well into a square yoke. Hand-made patchwork, including the clamshell pattern, can also be used (65, 66).

A variety of embroidery techniques were used by Dorothy Regler to decorate the unusual yoke of the dress in figure 67. Leather appliqué and

65 A patchwork jacket, with Seminole patchwork yoke. Designed by Angela Dewar.

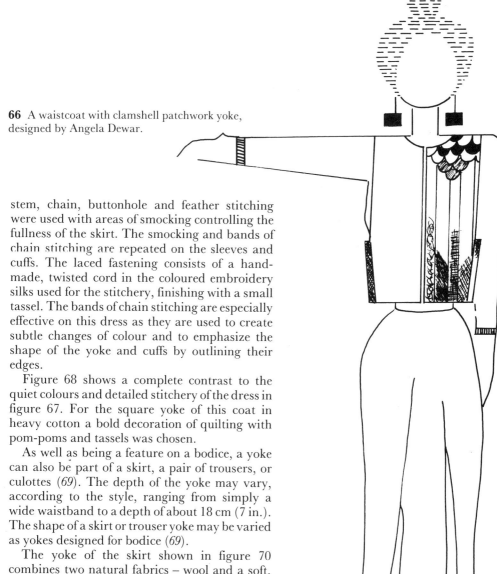

66 A waistcoat with clamshell patchwork yoke, designed by Angela Dewar.

stem, chain, buttonhole and feather stitching were used with areas of smocking controlling the fullness of the skirt. The smocking and bands of chain stitching are repeated on the sleeves and cuffs. The laced fastening consists of a hand-made, twisted cord in the coloured embroidery silks used for the stitchery, finishing with a small tassel. The bands of chain stitching are especially effective on this dress as they are used to create subtle changes of colour and to emphasize the shape of the yoke and cuffs by outlining their edges.

Figure 68 shows a complete contrast to the quiet colours and detailed stitchery of the dress in figure 67. For the square yoke of this coat in heavy cotton a bold decoration of quilting with pom-poms and tassels was chosen.

As well as being a feature on a bodice, a yoke can also be part of a skirt, a pair of trousers, or culottes (*69*). The depth of the yoke may vary, according to the style, ranging from simply a wide waistband to a depth of about 18 cm (7 in.). The shape of a skirt or trouser yoke may be varied as yokes designed for bodice (*69*).

The yoke of the skirt shown in figure 70 combines two natural fabrics – wool and a soft, washable gloving kid – as well as glass beads. A cord, hand-made from a skein of coton à broder, accentuates the yoke seam where it joins the main part of the skirt, and emphasizes the double points of this style. From these points hang four beaded and leather tasselled cords.

Leather work

Cutwork on leather has the advantage of the non-fraying qualities of this material, although it does have a tendency to stretch and should not be handled more than necessary. The design, as for all cutwork, must be very carefully worked out. (See page 51.)

4   A skirt, designed and made by Elizabeth Robertson. A fine, evenweave wool was used and each scalloped panel was worked separately, in needleweaving techniques. In the lower parts of the panels, the weft threads were withdrawn and replaced with a variety of textured threads and wools. Above this solid area of needleweaving are two rows of couched, variegated bouclé wool, repeating the scalloped shape. The skirt has a detachable belt, also decorated with needleweaving.

5   A woollen cloak with leather appliqué, designed and made by Gisela Banbury.

67 A woollen day dress, designed and made by Dorothy Regler. The unusual shaped yoke is decorated with leather appliqué, stem, chain, buttonhole and feather stitching.

68 Detail of a coat, in heavy cotton, designed and made by Mary Winnett.

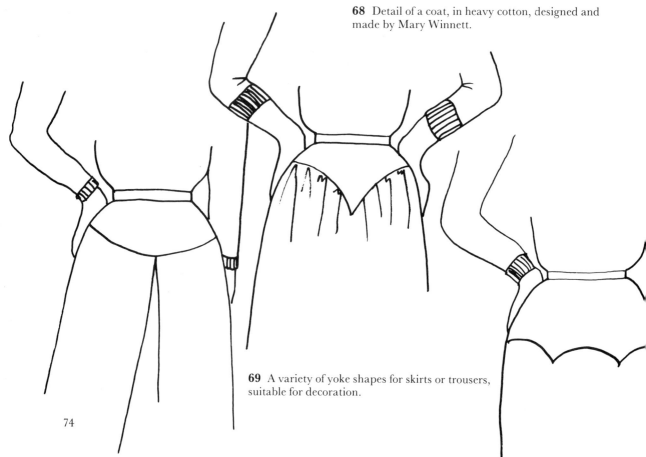

69 A variety of yoke shapes for skirts or trousers, suitable for decoration.

There are a few difficulties to be overcome when working on leather. To prevent finger or grease marks, we have found that a spray-on fabric protector can be an effective precaution, and sometimes even improves the appearance of the skin. Spray the whole skin before cutting out any of it. It will look alarmingly wet for a minute or two, but will soon dry out completely. The leather can then be handled with more confidence, but always work with clean hands. A sprinkling of talcum powder, rubbed very gently with a clean cloth over a small mark, will very often remove it.

Cutting out cannot be done in the normal way, using pins to attach the paper pattern, as these will permanently mark the skin with holes. The skin is also generally too thick to pin without stretching. Instead, one of the following two methods may be used and as it is an advantage to be able to see where the best part of the skin is, the second method may be preferable.

1 Place the skin right side down and lay the pattern onto the back of it. Draw around the pattern with a soft pencil and cut out.

2 Lay the skin right side up and select the best area. Lay the paper pattern onto the skin and stick it down with adhesive tape along the edges. Take care that the tape does not extend beyond the sewing line, as it will remove the 'bloom' of the leather when it is taken off. Cut out and peel away the tape.

Whichever method is used, remember to reverse the pattern if two pieces of the same shape are required, such as a pair of gloves or the right and left halves of a bodice.

Marking an embroidery design onto leather can only be done by the prick and pounce method (see page 14) or by drawing directly onto the skin, which may not be possible or wise.

The yoke in figure 70 was cut out in wool, leather and in thin calico. The leather and calico were fixed together with a light spraying of fixative (see page 130). This was done to help the leather to travel smoothly and it also acts as an interfacing for the yoke. (After making up, the calico seam allowance was trimmed away, as close to the stitching as possible.)

The embroidery design was stitched by machine onto the yoke, working over the design which was drawn in ink onto greaseproof paper. The paper design can be taped onto the leather, as described above, or can be held in place by several sliding paper clips around the edge. For stitching details, see page 56, notes 7-10). This method of sewing over greaseproof paper not only gives extra protection against a stray drop of oil from the machine, but also helps the leather to pass freely under the machine foot. Because the cut edges of leather do not fray, there was no need for any satin stitching, which, in this design, would have been impossible as it is too intricate to stitch in an even zigzag.

Once all the embroidery had been stitched the open parts of the design were cut away, near the stitching and at an even distance from it. The leather yoke was then mounted onto the woollen one, with spray-on adhesive.

The skirt was then made up. The zip fastener was placed in the centre back seam; an invisible type was chosen, which does not show if correctly inserted, and avoids extra sewing through the leather. The front and back of the skirt were made up separately and then joined at the side seams. All seams were pressed open, except those where the yoke joined the skirt. These were pressed up, towards the waist. Seam allowances were trimmed carefully, to avoid unnecessary bulk.

At this stage, the hand-made 'finger' cord was sewn along the seam line of the yoke and skirt, attaching two long cords at each point of the yoke. The cord was slip stitched invisibly, with a matching thread.

Because of the curved shape of the upper edge of the yoke, a facing was the most suitable way to finish the edge. A silk satin fabric was used for this, which makes the skirt easy to slip into. All seam allowances on the yoke section inside were hidden by the facing, which was neatly hemmed along the seam line.

Assorted glass beads, some smooth and some faceted, were sewn into the flower centres of the design and threaded onto the unknotted ends of the four long cords, putting on two extra as a foundation for the leather tassels. The last bead was knotted to secure it. The knot is hidden by the tassel.

To make a simple leather tassel (*71*), cut a strip of leather, approximately 10 cm (4 in.) by 4 cm (1½ in.). Cut one edge into a fine fringe, cutting to within 1 cm (⅜ in.) of the top. Smear a line of adhesive along the uncut edge and roll up the rectangle around the two last beads to form a tassel.

For a hand-knotted cord (or finger knitting)

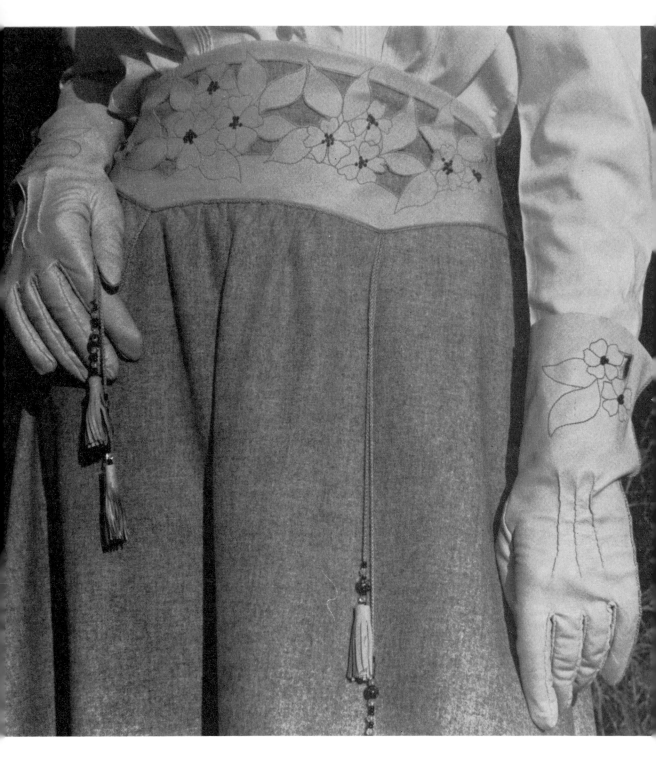

70 A woollen skirt, with leather cutwork yoke, designed and made by Angela Dewar. A hand-made cord accentuates the yoke seam. The flower motifs are highlighted with beads which are also included in the leather tassels hanging from the yoke. The design has been adapted on a pair of matching gloves.

the cord consists of two strands, looped together alternately (*72*):

1 Join the two strands together with a simple knot.

2 Form a twisted loop with the left-hand strand, as shown, with the long end of the strand underneath the short one. All following loops do not have to be twisted.

3 Push or pull a loop of the right-hand strand through the loop of the left-hand strand, and pull the left-hand strand tight.

4 Pull or push a loop of the left-hand strand through the loop of the right-hand strand and pull the right-hand strand tight.

Continue 3 and 4 until the cord is the required length. In figure 72 all loops are shown loose, to make it easier to follow the diagram. When the cord is worked, the strands should be pulled tight, as described in the instructions.

In figure 70 the model is wearing a pair of gloves which were made to match the embroidery on the skirt. The gloves were half made up, leaving the side seams open, to make working the embroidery more easy. A small part of the design from the skirt was used, and the method of working was exactly the same as for the skirt. The calico backing was trimmed away as much as possible when the embroidery was complete.

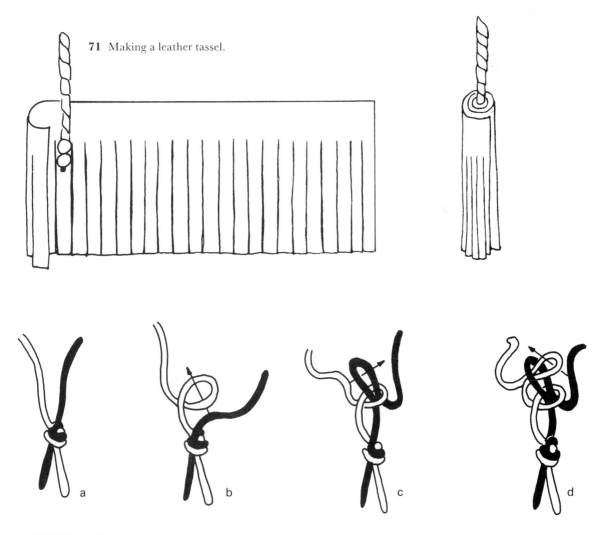

71 Making a leather tassel.

72 Making a finger cord.

6 Sleeves

The sleeve offers the embroiderer a much larger area and variety of style than any of those already mentioned. A study of historical portraits and costumes can result in several interesting ideas for decorating sleeves.

During the Tudor period sleeves were an important part of dress, for both men and women. Sometimes they were entirely separate from the bodice and were richly embroidered with metal threads and precious stones. Sometimes slashes were made in the top sleeve and 'puffs' of a soft undersleeve were pulled through. A portrait of Queen Elizabeth I suggested the idea for the sleeve in figure 74.

Cathedral window patchwork

Cathedral window patchwork has a strongly textured appearance and the combination of silk organza with beads in this example enriches it further. The patchwork must be made up into a piece, large enough to cut out the whole sleeve. The sleeve line should then be marked. This outline shape must be machined twice with small stitches just inside the cutting line to prevent the hand sewing and folding from coming undone (75). The sleeve can now be made up in the usual way, but stitch all seams twice and trim away excess fabric to 1 cm (3/8 in.); oversew by hand or machine.

Method

Basic cathedral window is a method of patchwork in which squares of fabric are folded several times into smaller squares and then sewn together by hand or machine (76). As for Somerset patchwork, the fabric should not be too springy or slippery, but it should hold a crease well. Cotton is easy to work with as are silks, especially when they are slightly stiff. The fabrics are always folded several times, which will make the finished piece rather thick and stiff if the fabric is too heavy. Sheer fabrics such as organdie make up into very interesting squares. The seams can then be covered up with a material of a different texture such as velvet. Very interesting patterns are created when striped fabrics are used.

1 Cut fabric squares measuring 12 cm by 12 cm (4¾ in. by 4¾ in.).

2 Turn 1 cm (3/8 in.) seam allowance on all four sides of the squares to the wrong side of the fabric. Press. If the fabric holds the fold easily there will be no need to tack the seam allowance.

3 Mark the centre of the square by folding it diagonally, first one way, then the other, and pressing the fold in the centre.

4 Place the square on the table wrong side up and fold all four corners to the centre mark. Press and hold in place with four straight stitches. The corners must be crisp and pointed.

5 If the patchwork is to be finished by hand then bring the needle and thread through the centre to the back of the square to keep it out of the way.

6 Fold the new corners of the smaller square to the centre in the same way as before.

7 Press gently, bring the needle and thread through the centre to the front and hold the new corners in place with four straight stitches or a cross stitch. Stitch through all layers of the fabric. Fasten the thread and cut off.

Join the patches in pairs by placing the right sides (folded sides) together and oversewing along one edge. Then join the pairs into rows. Join the rows together carefully, matching all seams.

If the patches are to be sewn together by machine (77) secure the four corners from the first folding with four straight stitches as described and fasten off the thread.

RIGHT
73 Elizabeth I (1533-1603) by Marcus Gheeraerts the Younger, c. 1592. (*National Portrait Gallery.*)

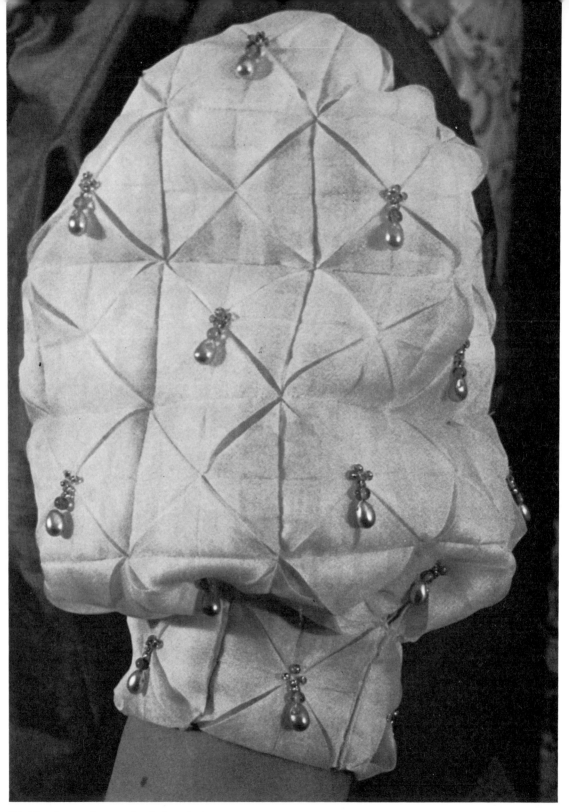

74 The sleeve of an evening jacket, designed and made by Gisela Banbury. The dress worn by Elizabeth I in figure 73 suggested the use of cathedral window patchwork for the sleeves. Silk organza was used for the patchwork which was further enriched by the addition of beads.

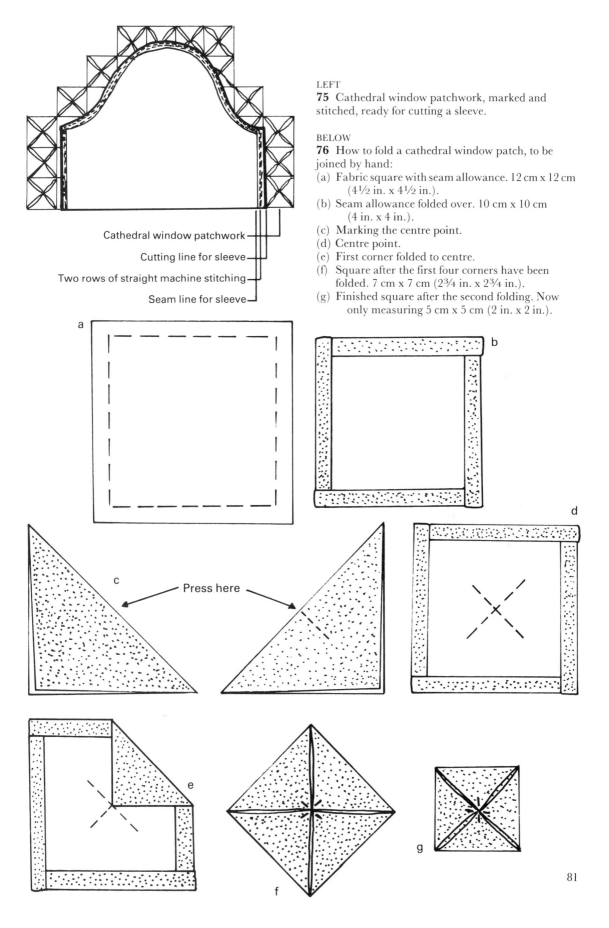

Cathedral window patchwork

Cutting line for sleeve

Two rows of straight machine stitching

Seam line for sleeve

LEFT
75 Cathedral window patchwork, marked and stitched, ready for cutting a sleeve.

BELOW
76 How to fold a cathedral window patch, to be joined by hand:
(a) Fabric square with seam allowance. 12 cm x 12 cm (4½ in. x 4½ in.).
(b) Seam allowance folded over. 10 cm x 10 cm (4 in. x 4 in.).
(c) Marking the centre point.
(d) Centre point.
(e) First corner folded to centre.
(f) Square after the first four corners have been folded. 7 cm x 7 cm (2¾ in. x 2¾ in.).
(g) Finished square after the second folding. Now only measuring 5 cm x 5 cm (2 in. x 2 in.).

Press here

81

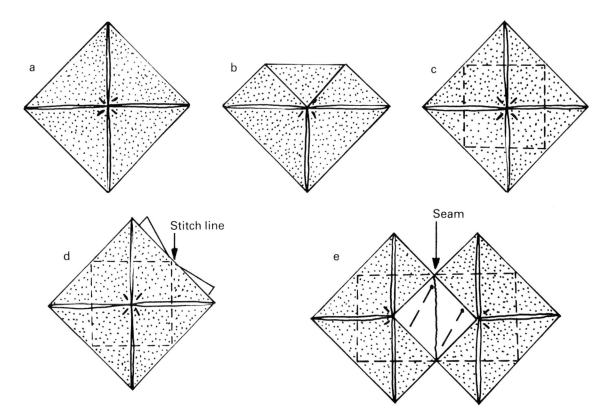

a

b

c

Stitch line

d

Seam

e

77 Cathedral window patchwork, joined by sewing machine:
(a) Patch as for hand sewing after the first folding.
(b) Fold each corner in turn, press but do not sew down.
(c) Stitch lines for machining.

Next fold the square again and press the edges to mark the fabric, but do not secure the corners to the centre of the patch; leave them loose.

Place two squares with their wrong (plain) sides together, matching the crease lines and stitching along one side.

Join all squares into pairs like this, then join the pairs into rows and so on.

Only after all the rows have been joined is it possible to secure the four corners of the second folding. They are fixed to the centre of the square with four straight stitches or one cross stitch. The stitches should go through all the layers of the fabric.

Basic cathedral window patchwork can be further embellished in a number of ways. Here are two variations:

1 (*78*) After the first folding and before the four corners are fixed to the centre of the large square, a piece of contrasting fabric can be inserted. It will be standing on its point and its centre should coincide with the centre of the large square. Now attach the four corners of the large square to the centre, as described, enveloping the inserted square. Continue as before. Later, when the slits of the finished squares are opened out as described below, the inserted contrasting fabric will be visible.

2 (*79*) Where two folded squares are joined together a smaller square is formed by two triangles, standing on its point and diagonally divided by the seam. This seam can be covered up with a square of the same or a contrasting fabric. The folded loose edges of the patchwork are then rolled back over the raw edges of the square and sewn down with slip stitch. The patchwork will be firmer if the slip stitches go all the way through to the back of the work. To make it easier to give the rolled-back edge of the squares a petal shape, the covering patch can be cut with curved sides. Iron-on vilene will give the patch more body and stop it fraying.

Beads can be sewn into the centres where the squares meet, but this is easier to do when the garment is finished.

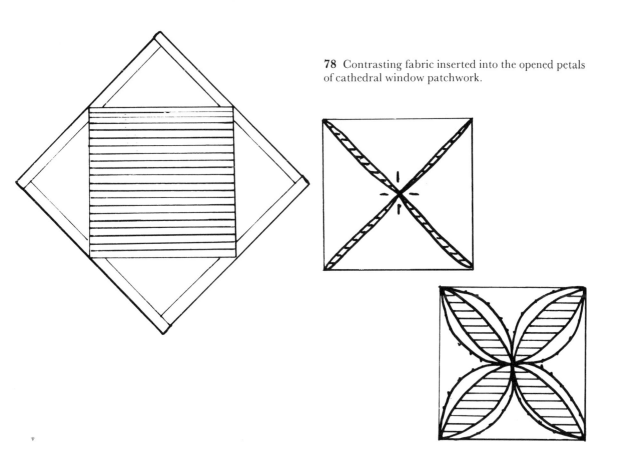

78 Contrasting fabric inserted into the opened petals of cathedral window patchwork.

79 Cathedral window patchwork, finished in the traditional way, with seams concealed by small fabric squares and folded, the loose edges rolled back and sewn down with slip stitch.

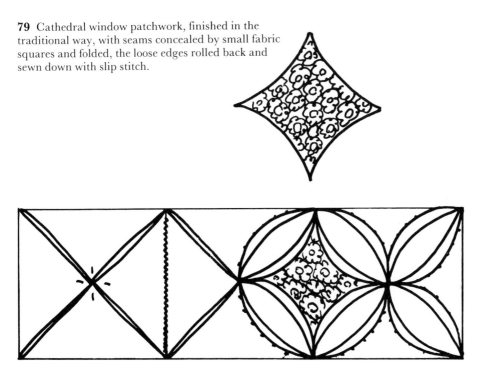

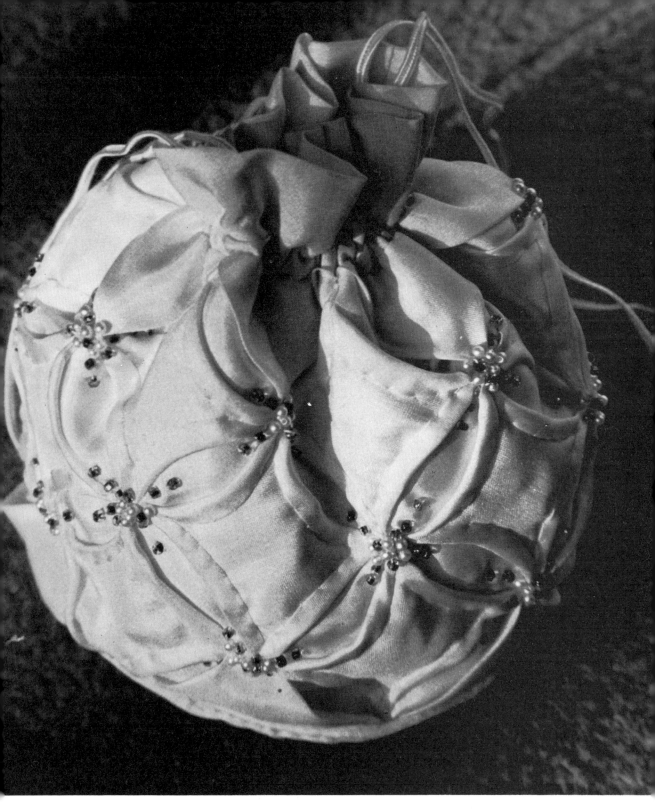

80 A bridesmaid's bag in traditional cathedral
window patchwork, made from white silk with small
gold beads and seed pearls.

81 The lower edge of the sleeve of an evening jacket, designed and made by Jennifer Stuart. In the floral design she used the following embroidery techniques: trapunto and Italian quilting, French knots, beading, appliqué and free machine embroidery.

Cathedral window patchwork is not suitable for everyday items, but is very effective on special projects like wedding dresses, bridesmaids' dresses, evening wear and accessories (*80*).

Quilting and appliqué

When time does not allow a large amount of embroidery to cover a garment, one smaller, very richly decorated section may be equally or more effective. A sleeve is a suitable area for such treatment but care should be taken to link the embroidery in some way with the rest of the garment. Figure 81 shows the lower section of the sleeve of an evening jacket embroidered by Jennifer Stuart. Although nearly all the work is placed on the sleeve, the same lines of Italian quilting are repeated on the bodice to create a border to the centre front edges, with one of the padded rose motifs also repeated at the neckline. The jacket is made of a brilliant turquoise silk and the techniques used for the embroidery include both trapunto and Italian quilting, free machine embroidery, straight machine stitching, beading and three-dimensional appliqué. Note how well the design fits into the shape of the sleeve, the heavy areas being in the lower part and the embroidery becoming lighter towards the narrowing sleeve head.

For high relief in trapunto quilting, the backing fabric must be firmer than the top fabric. A closely woven calico is generally suitable.

Preparing the fabric

1 Press the top and backing fabrics. Once the quilting is complete it is impossible to remove any bad creases from the surface.

2 Mark the design onto the top fabric (see page 14).

3 Tack the two layers of fabric together, working from the centre outwards for small pieces and in a square grid pattern for larger areas.

Machine stitching

1 Select a medium or long stitch. It is advisable to work a small trial piece first. For intricate corners and curves, a smaller stitch size may be more suitable.

2 Stitch over the design completely. Leave ends of at least 7 cm (3 in.) at the start and finish of each piece of stitching. This will facilitate secure

fastening off.

3 When the design has been stitched, draw all the threads through to the back of the work; tie and sew them firmly into the backing fabric.

Hand stitching

Stitch the design by hand, using small running stitches, back stitch or chain stitch.

Padding the design

1 Make a small slit in the backing fabric, in the areas which are to be padded.

2 Fluff out some fleece and insert it into the slit. Use the blunt end of a thick needle to push in the filling. Make sure that all corners are filled and that the padding is smooth on the front of the work. Do not overfill as this will cause the background to pucker.

3 When all the areas have been padded, draw the edges of the slits together with a loose overcasting stitch or lacing stitch.

Decoration for the sleeve head will also look more attractive if the embroidery is carried down the arm, avoiding an ugly, hard line. Figure 82 shows how a variety of purchased guipure lace motifs have been applied to the sleeve head and upper arm and bodice of a satin wedding dress. The appliqué was enriched by the addition of both hand and machine stitching and by three-dimensional butterflies.

82 Sue Tomkin's design for a wedding dress, using purchased guipure lace motifs, applied to the upper arm and bodice and combined with machine embroidery to the sleeve head.

7 Bodices

A bodice can present problems for the embroidery designer when it is fitted to the body by the use of darts. For this reason, it is advisable to choose a pattern which relies on the bust dart and side seam shaping only for the fit.

In patterns for men there is naturally no bust dart. However, in a garment such as the waistcoat in figure 83, the long dart, from the waistcoat point up to the chest, has been ignored completely. In a patchwork garment the design would be spoilt by the use of this dart, as it would break up the design of the patches. To make a new waistcoat pattern from a bought paper pattern, take a tracing of the waistcoat front but draw the bottom line from the centre front to the tip of the waistcoat point smoothly, ignoring the 'steps' of the dart. Continue to draw the bottom line smoothly from the waistcoat point to the side seam. This is now the new pattern (84).

Having chosen a suitable pattern for a woman's bodice, it is a good plan to make a toile, especially if the embroidery is complicated. The embroidery design may be pinned onto the toile to make sure that it is in the best possible position and the fit of the bodice can be checked. Any alterations on the toile should be transferred to the paper pattern, which is then used to cut out the garment. It is easier to work the embroidery before any darts are made and while the bodice is still flat. The shape of the dart must be transferred to the cloth with tailor's tacks and these shapes will be left empty. To make the design for a bodice proceed in the following way (85):

1 Take a tracing of the bought pattern.

2 Draw or trace the design onto the traced pattern, leaving the bust dart area empty.

3 Close the bust dart with pins to ensure that the design will look right when the edges of the dart are touching. If it does not, some adjustment to the design is necessary.

4 Make up the toile and pin on the design. Mull

83 Hand-made patchwork gentleman's waistcoat in silks and Liberty lawns, designed and made by Angela Dewar.

is a suitable fabric for the toile.

5 Check the fit and make any alterations.

It is always worth spending time to make an accurate design at this stage and so avoiding disappointment later.

Bodices which are not fitted, such as blousons or shirt-styles, are easier for the embroiderer to design as the area remains flat. However, the overall shape should still be considered at the design stage.

Most embroidery techniques are suitable for bodice decoration, although thought should be given to the wearing qualities of some methods when they are to be used in areas where friction may occur, such as between the arm and the side of the upper bodice or across the back. If the bodice of a garment is to have sleeves, a collar or a skirt attached to it, these must be taken into consideration when designing the embroidery. It is impractical to embroider the bodice where it would be covered by a collar. Embroidery on the sleeve, if any, should be in a position which does not conflict with the bodice embroidery. A large, flowing sleeve may cover the bodice to some extent and may not be suitable if the embroidery on the bodice is small or very subtle. No part of a garment should be embroidered thoughtlessly. The design on a bodice may be repeated on other parts of a garment, but the scale may have to adjusted.

84 How to adapt a commercial paper pattern for a waistcoat, to make it more suitable for embroidery.

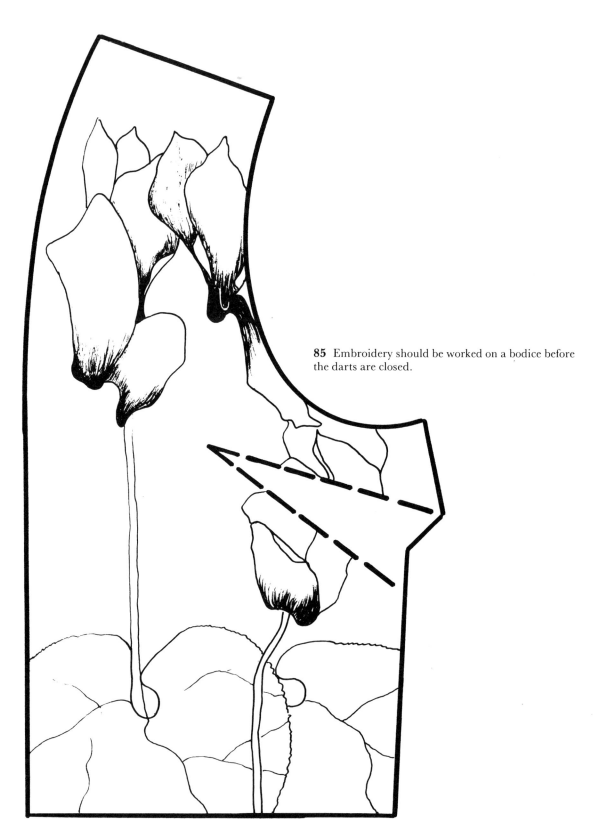

85 Embroidery should be worked on a bodice before the darts are closed.

Smocking

Smocking is a traditional form of embroidery which has been popular in Britain for many years. It is used to decorate the bodice, yoke and sleeve areas of clothes, both for women and men. Smocking is a simple technique based on the distribution of fabric into evenly gathered tubes, which are held in place with decorative surface stitches. The success of the smocking depends upon the even gathering of the fabric in the first place and on the choice of the colour scheme and stitches. Old smocks were made of linen, which made the gathering up easy as it was done by counting and picking up the threads of the fabric. For many years dotted transfers have been available, and they can now be bought in 12 different spacing sizes. These can be ironed onto the wrong side of printed or plain fabrics to ensure even gathering. Widely spaced dots will result in a smocked area one-third of its original width, so allow an amount of fabric at least three times the desired finished width. More of the fabric will be required if it is very fine, such as voile or a Liberty Tana lawn. Spotted fabrics can be used without the help of a transfer, if the spacing of the dots is suitable. Make sure that the material has been cut straight when using spotted fabric in this way, otherwise the rows of smocking will slant.

The quickest form of smocking is honeycombing. A modern example of this can be seen in figure 86. This approach to a traditional craft adds both interest and elegance to a simple dress; the deep V of the embroidery makes a change from the usual straight-edged appearance.

Little girls have long been dressed in pretty smocked dresses, which have become a tradition in themselves (*87*).

A traditional working smock style can be fun to make and wear today (*88*). Made long in silk, it can be worn for formal evenings and in cotton, linen or viyella as a casual partner for trousers or jeans. It is particularly suitable for maternity wear, being both attractive and comfortable. As with all techniques, it is a good idea to make a small trial piece first.

86 A woollen day dress with honeycomb smocking, designed by Anna Roose for Celtic Fringe.

87 A seed cotton child's dress, with traditionally smocked bodice, designed and made by Jane Smith.

88 A modern version of a traditional working smock, designed and made by Jane Smith.

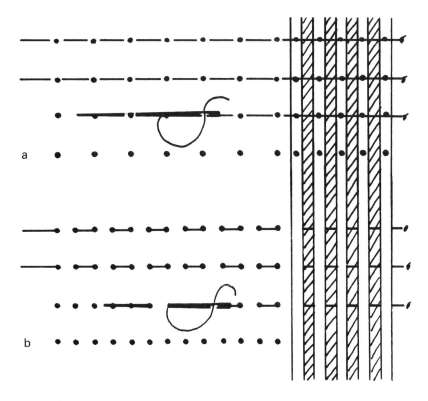

89 (a) Gathering the fabric in preparation for smocking. A small amount of fabric is picked up with each dot, until the row is complete.
(b) Gathering fabric in preparation for smocking. The needle is inserted in the first dot and brought out in the next, until the row is completed.

Preparing the cloth

1 Select the chosen transfer.

2 Place the transfer, shiny side down, onto the wrong side of the fabric, making sure that the dots are perfectly on the straight grain of the cloth. Do not pin or tack the transfer paper around the edge as this can distort it and result in an uneven distribution of dots. If necessary on a large area, tack the transfer once down the centre and then once across the width. A warm iron and a firm pressure are needed to ensure that each dot is transferred. Lift a corner to check that the transfer is a success before tearing away the paper.

3 Choose a strong polyester thread to make the gathers. Silk thread should be used for silk fabric. Each line of dots needs a piece of thread the length of the fabric to be gathered, plus approximately 15 cm (6 in.). Make a large knot in one end of the gathering thread.

4 Working from right to left, insert the needle into the first dot, bring it out at the next and continue until the row is finished. Carry on in the same way until all the rows are done (*89a*). (We find this to be a quicker and more accurate method of gathering the fabric than the more widely practised way of picking up each dot. For

this method a close spacing of dots is necessary (*89b*).)

5 To pull up the gathers, work on a pair of threads at a time, holding the fabric steady with one hand and pulling gently with the other. When all the pairs have been pulled up and the gathered tubes are lying closely together, stroke them with the eye of the needle to tidy them and make them even. Let the tubes relax and distribute themselves evenly to a width a little less than the finished work will be, as smocking gives elasticity to the finished fabric.

6 To fasten the gathering threads securely, insert a pin vertically at the end of each pair of rows. Cut off all except the last 15 cm (6 in.) of the gathering thread. Wind this around the pin in a figure of eight. On very lightweight materials, put the spare threads into the eye of a needle and secure them with one or two back stitches.

Stitches

Some of the traditional smocking stitches such as stem or outline stitch, cable stitch, Vandyke stitch (worked from right to left) and their variations, give a tighter finish than the more recently developed chevron stitch or honeycomb stitch. For this reason a combined arrangement

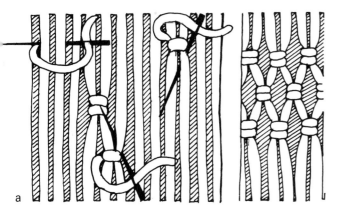

90 Traditional smocking stitches:
(a) Honeycomb stitch.
(b) Single cable stitch.
(c) Chevron stitch.
(d) Double cable stitch.
(e) Stem or outline stitch.
(f) Vandyke stitch.

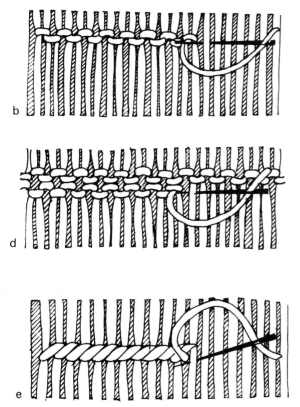

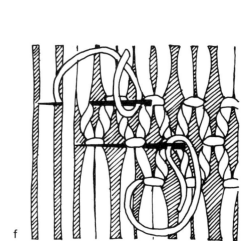

of these stitches must be carefully planned. Where any strain in likely to occur, such as the lower rows of smocking on a child's garment, it is preferable to use the more elastic stitches such as chevron or surface honeycomb stitch, and honeycomb stitch.

The top row of smocking is usually worked in cable or outline stitch. There are many fascinating and beautiful smocking patterns to be found on garments in private collections and museums and original designs can easily be derived from these by the embroiderer with an eye for pattern.

The smocking should be worked from left to right and the thread must be long enough to complete each row of stitching. It is not advisable to join in a fresh piece of thread in the middle of a row as this looks ugly on the back of the work and causes an uneven appearance on the front.

When all the rows of smocking are complete, and before the gathering threads are removed, place the work, face down, on the ironing table. Using a steam iron (or a damp cloth and ordinary iron), steam the smocking with the least possible pressure, passing the iron over the work once or twice. This 'sets' the pleats and raises the smocking stitches.

After the eighteenth century traditional smocks nearly always had areas of additional surface embroidery. The shoulder bands, collar, cuffs and the 'box' area, which is on either side of the smocked panel on the front and back of the smock, were covered with embroidery. The patterns used include leaves, scrolls, flowers, hearts and cones and are believed by some to denote the trade of the original wearer. Each county had its own patterns, many of them very intricate; sometimes they were combined with tucking to give a very rich texture.

Some of the surface stitches used in traditional smock embroidery are: herringbone stitch, feather stitch, back stitch and chain stitch.

A traditional motif from an old smock has been used to decorate the bodice of the dress illustrated in figure 92.

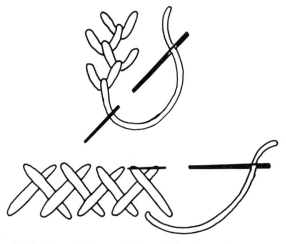

91 Surface stitches used in traditional smock embroidery: feather stitch and herringbone stitch.

Detachable bodices

One way of making a dress a more versatile garment is to make a detachable overbodice. If the dress itself is plain and usually worn informally, it can be made into a special occasion garment when worn with its embroidered overbodice. This is very simple in shape, without any darts, and can either be slipped over the head and fastened at the waistline, or can have a shoulder fastening which can be made into a decorative feature.

It is easy to design for this uncomplicated flat area. Asymmetrical patterns are more unusual. Figure 96 shows an overbodice design of simple triangle shapes. The shapes have been allowed to overlap and parts of the resulting pattern are solid and worked in appliqué. The appliqué can be stitched on by machine as this will be concealed by the outline of threads or cords which are couched around the whole design (*93*).

Machine embroidery

An asymmetrical design, suggested by sketches of trees, was chosen to decorate the bodice of a black georgette evening dress (*94*). The embroidery was worked onto the fabric before the dress was cut out. First, vertical twin needle tucks were made, the lines of stitching growing longer as the tucking progressed across the bodice, being approximately 15 cm (6 in.) long from the right shoulder point and 42 cm (16 in.) long from the left shoulder point. The fabric was then put into a tambour frame. A thick, black cotton crochet thread was used in the spool of the machine, and tree shapes were stitched among the tucks, using a free machine embroidery technique and working on the wrong side of the fabric. It is sometimes necessary to remove the tension screw and spring from the spool case when a thick thread is being used. This allows the thread to pass freely through the hole in the side of the spool case. The tension screw and spring are very small and care should be taken to store them in a safe place. Many machine embroiderers keep a separate spool case for their

---

RIGHT
92 A traditional motif from an old smock has been used to decorate the bodice of a woollen dress. Designed by Anna Roose for Celtic Fringe.

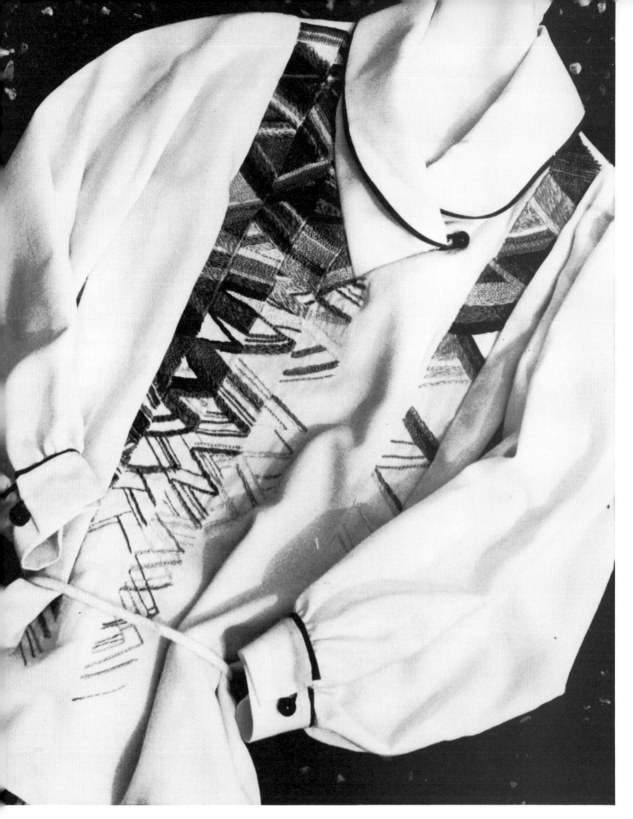

93 A blouse in Liberty challis designed and made by Grace Grant. The asymmetrical design was worked in chain stitch, using a variety of yarns, and in a range of blues and turquoise, on a cream ground.

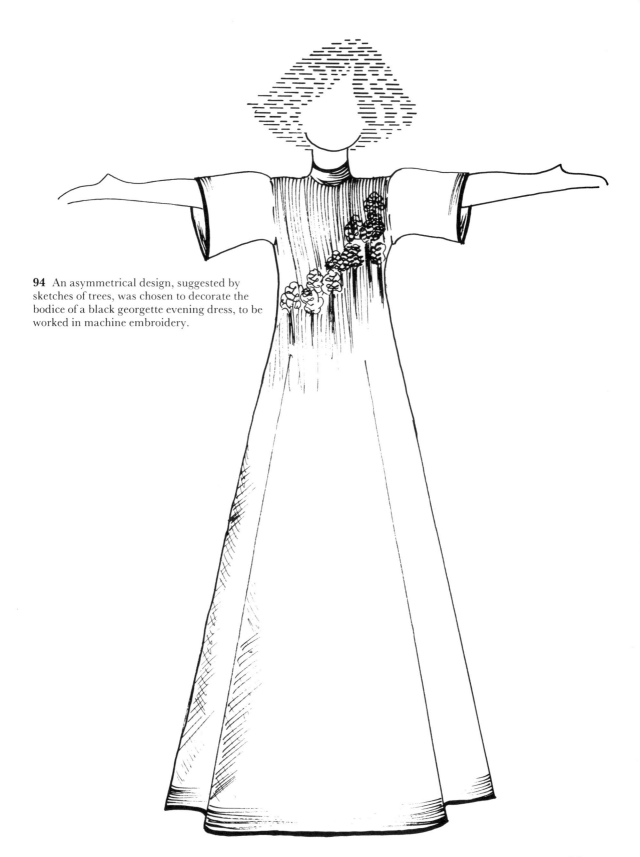

94 An asymmetrical design, suggested by sketches of trees, was chosen to decorate the bodice of a black georgette evening dress, to be worked in machine embroidery.

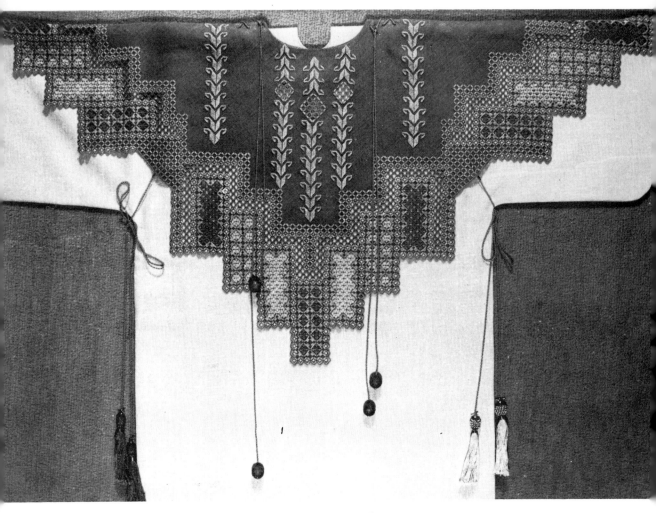

95 Detachable bodice (in Hardanger work) by Heide Jenkins.

embroidery as it is not always easy to return to the perfectly correct tension required for ordinary sewing.

After the machine embroidery was completed, the dress was cut out and made up and jet beading was added to the design, by hand. To finish the dress, the hems of the skirt and the bell-shaped sleeves were bound in black silk satin and a border of twin needle tucks, approximately 10 cm (4 in.) deep, was added. The neck edge was finished with a stand-up collar of horizontally tucked fabric, bound with black silk satin.

Jackets

The bodice area of a jacket is not usually as closely fitted as that of a dress, as it is designed to wear over another garment. Designing and making a jacket for a child can be rewarding exercise, as children are less inhibited than adults about wearing 'fun' clothes. The embroiderer can use her imagination as much as she likes, with bold use of pattern and colour, and ingenuity of design.

Examples of jackets for children can be seen in colour plate 1 and figure 97. Sue Tomkins designed and made the 'jungle' jacket for her ten-year-old daughter as one of the pieces of work for the City & Guilds Embroidery Examination, Part II. The jacket is made of a bright blue wool and the jungle scene is worked in a variety of surface stitches. Notice how the design has been

made to fit well into the shape of the jacket front. Parts of the design have been allowed to stray onto the upper sleeve, thus avoiding a 'cut off' appearance and adding charm and spontaneity to the whole. In the same way, the design flows over the side seams and the scene is elaborated on the back of the jacket, with a striped tiger peering through the leafy ferns and trees.

This jacket demonstrates a modern use of the familiar crewel work techniques found on embroideries of many periods. From the time of the Bayeux Tapestry, of the wool-embroidered Jacobean hangings of the seventeenth and eighteenth centuries and of William Morris in the nineteenth century, the embroiderer has used the beauty of richly dyed woollen yarns to decorate her surroundings and her clothes, and there is certainly no reason why she should not continue to do so today. A wide range of crewel wools is available, both from shops and through mail order services. The anorak shown in figure 97 was also a piece of work made during a City & Guilds Embroidery course. Kate King chose a biege needlecord for the anorak for a one-year-old grandchild. Clever use has been made of the zip fastener by attaching a small brown felt mouse to the pull tag. The mouse runs up and down a brown needlecord 'clock' applied to the centre front of the garment, in two parts on either side of the zip opening. The clock face is worked in one piece, stitched to the right front and fastened with touch-and-close fastener on the left front. The 'hickery, dickery dock' theme from the nursery rhyme is continued on the rest of the garment, which is quilted all over in a pattern of mice, each one emphasized with a couched, brown cord.

When making a garment such as this, it is important to plan the construction and the order of working before a start is made. This will help to avoid frustrating mistakes and will greatly add to the pleasure of creating an original design.

A simple way of decorating a small child's bolero is shown in figure 98. Here, the crocodiles and elephants printed onto the border of an Indian silk have been worked in English quilting with the addition of a few French knots. The idea for this piece of work was suggested by the fabric

---

96 An asymmetrical design for an overbodice, to be worked in appliqué and couching.

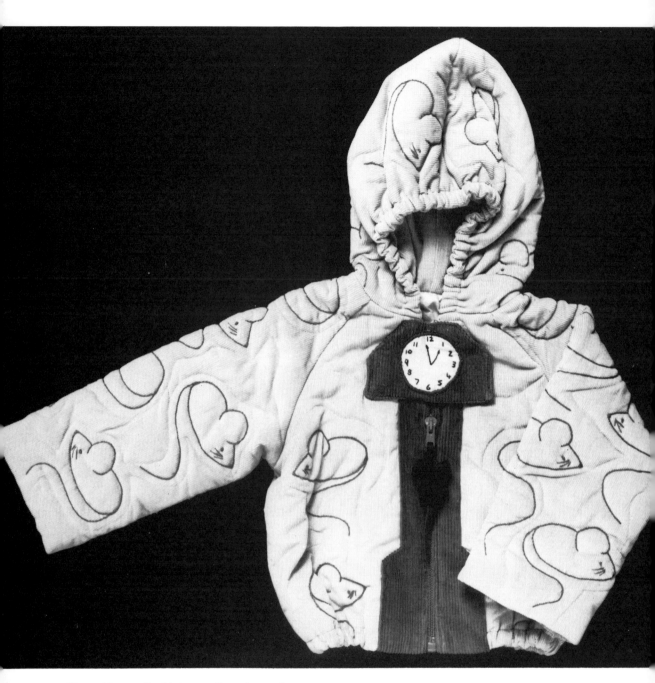

97 A child's quilted beige needlecord anorak, designed and made by Kate King. Clever use has been made of the zip fastener by attaching a small, brown felt mouse to the pull tag. The mouse runs up and down a brown needlecord 'clock' applied to the centre front of the garment.

RIGHT
98 A small child's bolero, decorated with quilted and embroidered crocodiles and elephants.

itself and this can be a good way for a beginner to make a start on embroidery for clothing, as there are so many attractive printed fabrics available. A clear, simple design will give more satisfying results than a fussy print.

Combined techniques

Quilting can be successfully combined with either patchwork (*99*) or with fabric painting or spray dyeing (*100*). The design for figure 100 was derived from a simplified sketch of a piece of driftwood. Several tracings of the sketch were made, altering and correcting lines and curves, until a pleasing shape and suitable size evolved. More tracing paper was used to reverse and repeat the design so that it fitted the back and the front of the waistcoat. Tracing paper is very useful to the embroiderer who feels the lack of confidence or ability to draw to a high standard, as tracings may be taken from many sources if an original sketch is not available. Patterns can also be created by folding and cutting paper and taking tracings of the resulting shapes. Always bear the size and shape of the garment in mind when choosing motifs for fashion embroidery. After a little practice, designs will begin to suggest themselves from a variety of source materials. Instructions for enlarging designs are given in on page 13.

For painting on fabrics there is a variety of media available from local shops or by mail order

99 A design for a waistcoat, combining patchwork and quilting.

(see Suppliers' page 142). Transfer paints or pencils are simple to use. The design is put onto paper before being transferred to the fabric with an iron. Any mistakes can be cut out or touched up at this stage. However, some experiments with the colours should be made, as the paints react differently on each type of fabric. Colours are much stronger when used on man-made fabrics, such as polyester. Usually these paints and dyes are sold with instructions included.

100 A design for a waistcoat, derived from studies of a piece of driftwood, suitable for the combined techniques of fabric painting and quilting.

8 Skirts

Embroidery for a skirt has a range of possibilities. The techniques chosen will depend largely on the purpose of the skirt and, of course, its style. Is the skirt part of a dress? Is it designed to wear with a particular blouse or jacket? Perhaps it is tempting for a beginner to 'play safe' and to opt for a rather cautious approach, such as a quiet border or a motif for a pocket, and while these can be attractive it is much more exciting to try a bolder design. Always take the silhouette and length of the skirt into consideration, to achieve a balanced design.

Seam decoration and border design have already been discussed in previous chapters. Some of the ideas suggested are suitable for use on skirts.

The skirt in colour plate 4, designed and worked by Elizabeth Robertson, was made from a fine, evenweave woollen fabric and lined with silk. Each scalloped panel was worked separately in needleweaving. In the lower part of the panels, the weft threads of the fabric were withdrawn and replaced with a variety of textured threads and wools. Above this solid area of needleweaving are two rows of couched variegated bouclé wool, repeating the scalloped shape. The belt is also needlewoven and is detachable.

Although clothes for formal daytime occasions should generally not be too elaborate, clever use of colour and shape can transform a plain woollen skirt, with a matching jacket, into an unusual and elegant outfit. A visit to any museum of costume will certainly stimulate some good ideas for decorating modern dress. The Victorians were fond of using braid to decorate their clothes and an up to date interpretation of this method is suggested in figure 101.

We are accustomed to thinking of patchwork in terms of cotton prints and silks but it can be equally effective when worked in tweeds and velvets. This use of small remnants of fabric is a reminder of the original purpose of patchwork. Instructions for making up a 16-panel skirt in patchwork on a plain yoke are given below:

Patchwork skirt

A commercial A-line pattern was used for this skirt. The fabrics came from two old pairs of corduroy trousers, one pair of woollen ones, two plain skirts and one pair of pyjamas. The lining was new fabric.

Cut the lining and waistband according to the pattern. Divide the paper pattern into a 20 cm (8 in.) deep yoke and skirt section. The dividing line should follow the curve of the waistline. Add 1 cm (½ in.) seam allowance to the yoke. Make up the yoke, inserting the zip fastener at the left side. Make up the lining, leaving open 18 cm (7 in.) on the left side. Tack the lining to the yoke at the waistline, wrong sides together. Make up and apply the waistband. Neatly hem stitch the opening in the lining to the zipper tapes. The skirt is now ready to have the patchwork attached to it.

To make the patchwork, fold the skirt part of the paper pattern in half and then fold it twice more. Press the folds well. When the paper is opened out the fold lines will have divided the pattern into eight equal panels. Any one of these can be used as a pattern for the 16 panels from which the skirt is made up (103).

Add 5 cm (2 in.) to the hem line of the chosen panel (104). Shape the top edge of the chosen panel to a right-angled point and mark the grain line down the centre of the panel. Cut the panel into a number of triangles and rhomboids as in figure 104.

To make the paper shapes into templates for machine patchwork, stick them onto a large piece of card, well spaced out. Add a seam allowance of 1 cm (½ in.) to each side of each patch and cut these templates from the card. Sixteen patches have to be cut from each template. Mark and cut them very carefully, with the grain line following the centre line of the panel, as marked.

101 A design for an outfit in wool with applied braid.

102 A design for a 16-panel patchwork skirt, made from remnants of wool, corduroy and brushed cotton.

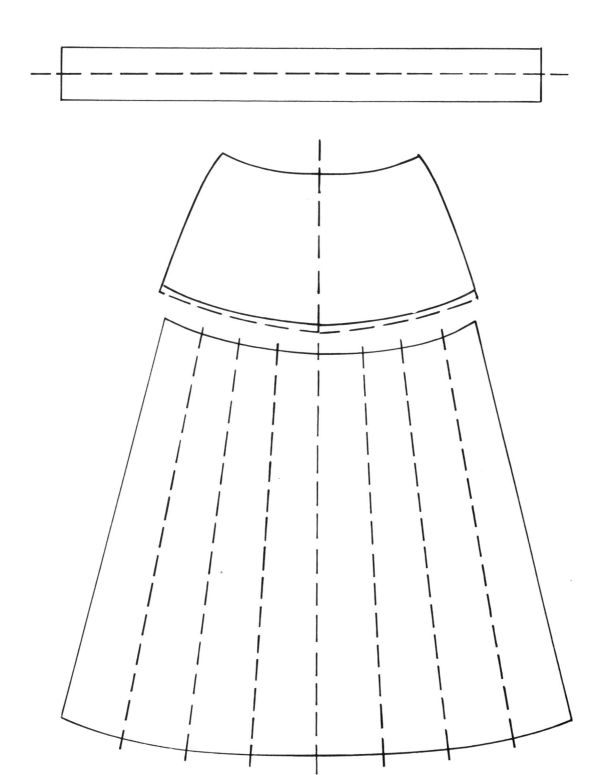

103 Division of the paper pattern to make the skirt in
figure 102.

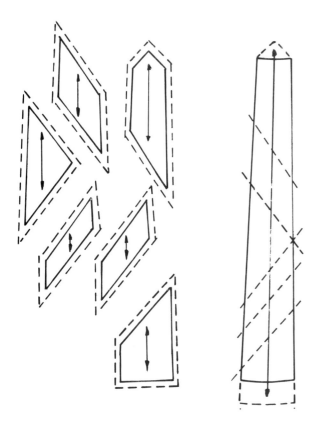

104 Any skirt panel from figure 102 can be divided and made into patchwork templates.

The darkest coloured fabric should be chosen for the patches on the hem of the skirt. The patches at the top edge of the skirt part are cut from the same fabric as the yoke, so that the join over the hips is not unnecessarily emphasized. Machine the patches together, matching the cut edges carefully and taking a 1 cm (½ in.) seam allowance. Make up all 16 panels. Press open all the seams. Join all the panels by machine, starting to sew 1 cm (½ in.) from the top, again taking care to match the edges and with the 1 cm (½ in.) seam allowance. Press all these vertical seams in one direction. Fold and tack under the seam allowance on the top edge, forming a zigzag line. Tack this to the yoke and top stitch. Adjust the hem line and work the hem.

Pleated skirts

Pleated skirts may appear to be more difficult to embellish than plain ones, as the pleats themselves are a decorative feature of the style. However, there are ways of emphasizing the pleats, which will add to their attraction. Embroidery may be placed on the underside of pleats, so that it is glimpsed only during movement, or when the wearer is seated and the pleats fall open. Designs for this type of long, narrow decoration can, of course, be adapted from border designs. Remember that the underside of most flat pleats tapers towards the top and that any embroidery should follow the usual design principle of fitting the shape on which it is placed.

An alternative approach to pleat decoration is to embroider over the seam out of which it opens. The tailored 'sprats' head' arrow could be elaborated by repeating it in diminishing sizes towards the waistline. Small arrows, made of soft kid for example, might be applied to the top of pleats, instead of the more usual stitched sprats' heads.

Appliqué

Children's clothes for everyday wear should be quick and easy to make. As little girls grow so fast, it is pointless for busy mothers to spend too many precious hours on meticulous handwork. Special occasion garments, such as christening robes, embroidered or smocked party dresses or bridesmaids' outfits are the exceptions. A prettily decorated skirt for a small girl can quickly be made from an appliqué technique. Satin stitch on the sewing machine is easy to work with a little practice. Designs for appliqué should be simple in outline. A fussy edge will look confusing. Detail can be added at a later stage with hand embroidery or more machine stitching (*105*).

To prepare work for appliqué by machine proceed as follows:

1 Draw the design. Use tracing paper, if necessary, to repeat motifs or to arrange them into a pattern.

2 Select fabrics for the appliqué. Cotton on cotton is a good rule to follow, as it makes laundering easier. Stretchy materials are not at all suitable for appliqué, neither are fabrics which fray easily.

3 Choose a thread for the machine stitching. Machine embroidery thread is the most suitable.

4 When cutting out the appliqué pieces, the grain should match that of the background fabric. This will prevent wrinkles appearing in the finished work. If using fabric off the grain

105 A border of geese for the hem of a child's skirt. The design has been applied by machine, using satin stitch. The sample was worked by Frances Gibb.

---

cannot be avoided, a lightweight vilene (iron-on) should be used as a backing. Remember that this will stiffen the fabric considerably and change its character. Apply the backing before cutting out the appliqué shapes.

5 Tack the appliqué design carefully onto the background fabric.

6 Set the machine to satin stitch. Make a trial sample before working on the garment. Adjust the stitch width and length, if necessary. When zigzag stitching, the needle should pierce the appliqué fabric on one side and the background material on the other. Turning corners should be done by leaving the needle in the work, lifting the pressure foot and pivoting the cloth. Replace the presser foot and continue stitching. Practise turning corners on the trial sample. Beginners will find curved shapes easier to work than tight circles or sharp corners.

The waistband edge of a simple skirt can be shirred for ease of wearing and to allow for an expanding waistline.

To lengthen children's skirts decoratively, a width of contrasting fabric can be let into the garment, near the hem. The seams of the inserted fabric can be decorated as described on page 18.

Surface stitchery

In contrast to the appliqué skirt described above, the party dress (*back cover*) demonstrates what can be done when more time is available. The blue-spotted, white voile fabric was used as the basis for the embroidery design. The spots are used to make the centres of small flower heads, worked in a variety of surface stitches (*106*). The number of flowers gradually increases towards the hemline (*107*). The strands of a stranded cotton thread were used for the embroidery, in shades of blue, ranging from light to dark. A row of flowers is also worked across the yoke of the frock, where it joins the skirt, increasing in size at the centre. This balances the weight of the embroidered skirt and conceals the seam turning on the translucent fabric.

109

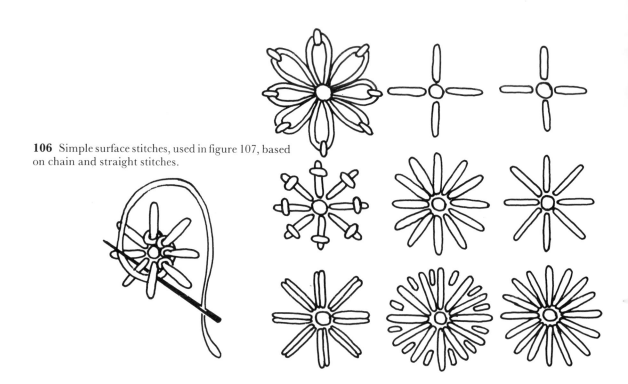

106 Simple surface stitches, used in figure 107, based on chain and straight stitches.

107 Detail of the party dress shown on the back cover.

9 Clothes for special occasions

For everyday clothes the first thought should alway be practicality; no such considerations are necessary for garments made for a special occasion. No christening gown or evening dress is expected to be practical; they should first of all look beautiful, festive and original. For imaginative embroiderers, these are ideal projects to develop ideas and practise skills.

Christening robes

Instructions are given below for making the christening dress in figure 108. A fine cotton/polyester lawn was used for the dress. The drawn thread work and tucks were worked by hand with white machine embroidery thread, no. 50. The flowers were worked in bullion knots, detached chain and back stitch, using a white perlé, no. 8.

Choose a commercial pattern for a simply styled baby gown, with yoke, short puffed sleeves and straight skirt gathered into the yoke. The length of the skirt can be varied.

Cut out the dress as instructed in the pattern. The drawn thread border along the hem of the skirt should be worked first. Withdraw threads as shown in figure 110. The first thread is always tricky to remove, especially on a fine fabric. Pick up one thread with the tip of a needle and gently ease it out of the fabric, across the width of the skirt. A magnifying glass may be helpful.

Turn the fabric to the wrong side, along the first withdrawn thread, near the bottom edge. Press it along the fold and, again folding to the wrong side, match the folded edge to the bottom edge of the first band of withdrawn threads, forming a hem 4 cm (1½ in.) deep. Tack and press the hem as shown in figure 111a. Working on the wrong side of the fabric and stitching from left to right, secure the folded hem, whilst working the first border of zigzag hem stitch. Hem stitch is usually worked over an even number of warp threads, four or six, according to the thickness of the fabric.

To start, secure the working thread invisibly into the fold of the hem and bring it to the front of the work two threads below the fold of the hem, as shown in figure 111b.

Count four (six) warp threads to the right and insert the needle from right to left, picking up the four warp threads and bringing the needle to the front of the work again, just above the starting point (111c).

Pull the working thread tight towards the hem to gather the four warp threads into a bundle. Insert the needle from the back of the work, bringing it to the front on the right of the bundled threads and two weft threads below the edge of the withdrawn border as shown in figure 111d. To secure the hem at the same time, take the needle also through the folded hem, two weft threads below the fold. Count the next four threads to the right, and pick them up from left to right as before. Pull the working thread tight, to bundle the threads and, as before, anchor the working thread with a small stitch, two weft threads deep and on the right of the new bundle, including the folded hem.

Succeeding rows of hem stitching will have no folded hem to be attached and therefore will only be stitched through a single layer of fabric.

When the bottom edge of the band of zigzag hem is complete, turn the skirt upside down and work the upper edge of the same band, still on the wrong side of the skirt and from left to right, dividing the bundles and joining the second half of one to the first half of the next. On this edge there is no folded hem in which the stitching and finishing off of the working thread may be hidden and therefore the thread ends must be woven neatly into the fabric, between the first and second horizontal threads.

For a ladder hem (111e), the same four threads will be bundled together on the upper and lower edges of the band.

To make the twisted borders (111f), first work a completed row of ladder hem. Next, secure a

LEFT
108 A christening robe, designed and made by
Angela Dewar.

109 Detail of the border of the christening robe
shown in figure 108, showing hand-worked pin-tucks,
rows of hem stitching and rosebuds embroidered in
bullion knots.

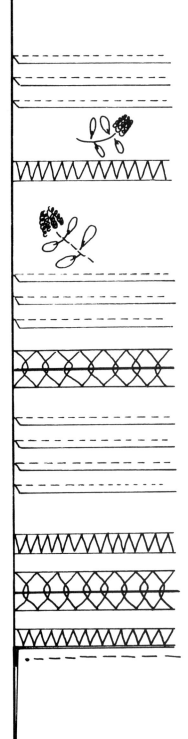

length of strong working thread (perlé 8), a little longer than the width of the skirt, into the right edge of the skirt, in the centre of the ladder hem. Work from right to left. Count two bundles to the left. Insert the needle after the second bundle and turn it to the right, bringing it up between the first and second bundles. Take the needle over the first bundle and turn it back to the left, taking the first bundle with it and placing it to the left of the second bundle. Pull the working thread through. Continue to twist the remainder of the ladder hem in the same way and secure the working thread firmly into the left-hand edge of the skirt. Make sure that it is not pulled too tight.

When all the bands of hem stitching are finished, according to figure 110, turn the skirt to the right side, to work the tucks.

Fold and lightly press the fabric along the lines where single threads have been withdrawn and hold the folds by working small running stitches through the two layers of fabric, 2 mm (⅛ in.) away from and parallel to the fold.

Using perlé no. 8 thread, work small flowers between some of the bands, as shown in figure 110. These consist of five bullion knots (*112*) for the rosebuds, back stitch for the stems and detached chain stitches for the leaves.

Work bullion knot roses on the front of the yoke, spaced as in figure 108.

Withdraw a band of threads 0.5 cm (³⁄16 in.) wide, 1 cm (⅜ in.) from the lower edge of the sleeve. Fold the narrowest possible double hem, match it to the lower edge of the withdrawn band and secure with ladder hem stitching.

Make five vertical pin-tucks, 2.5 cm (1 in.) long, at the sleeve head.

Make up the dress, either by hand or by machine. Keep excess bulk in the seams to a minimum. Thread a narrow, cotton braid or ribbon through the ladder hem stitching at the lower edge of the sleeve and tie in a bow. Top stitch around the neck edge, by hand.

Another christening robe can be seen in figures 113 and 114. This delicate and unusual dress was made by Mary Tasker. She chose to use organza, metal thread and a little lurex. The design is reminiscent of the Art Nouveau period and is worked in shadow quilting and tucks. The edge is scalloped and hand-finished in buttonhole stitch worked with a thin lurex thread. The design is worked on the skirt, with a variation on a smaller scale repeated on the yoke.

110 Arrangement of pin-tucks and hem stitching on the christening robe in figure 108.

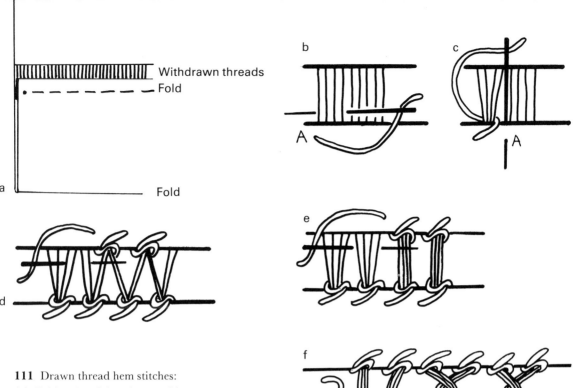

111 Drawn thread hem stitches:

(a) Fold and tack hem into position.

(b) Work from left to right. Secure the working thread in the fold of the hem and bring it out at A. Pick up a bundle of threads with the needle, as shown.

(c) To secure the previous stitch, take the needle to the back of the work to the right of the bundled threads and bring it out at point A, the starting point for the next stitch.

(d) To complete a zigzag hem, bundle and secure the threads as shown, joining half of one bundle with half of the neighbouring bundle.

(e) For a ladder hem, the same group of threads will be bundled on the upper and lower edges of the band.

(f) For a twisted border, first work a row of ladder hem. Next, secure a length of strong working thread (perlé 8), a little longer than the border, into the right edge of the border, in the centre of the ladder hem. Work from right to left. Count two bundles to the left. Insert the needle after the second bundle and turn it to the right, bringing it up between the first and second bundles. Take the needle over the first bundle and turn it back to the left, taking the first bundle with it and placing it to the left of the second bundle. Pull the working thread through and continue to twist the remainder of the hem in the same way, securing the working thread into the left edge of the border when it is finished.

112 Bullion knot stitch.

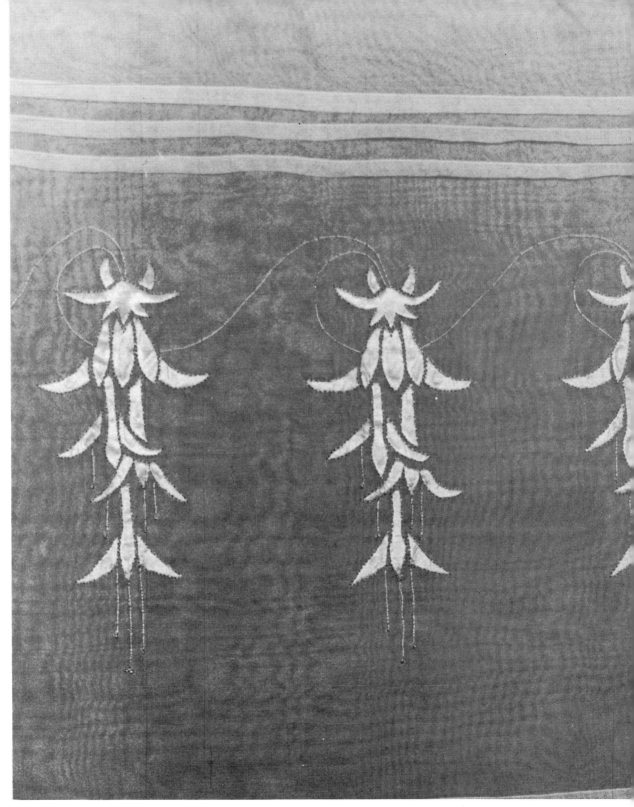

113 A christening robe, designed and made by Mary Tasker.

114 Detail of the robe in figure 113. The design is worked in shadow quilting with tucks, on organza with metal threads and a little lurex.

Weddings

The making of a wedding dress is a challenge to any dressmaker and embroiderer. A wedding gown is not just one article, but a piece in a jigsaw puzzle, where many components have to fit together to make up the bridal picture. It is therefore a good idea to leave plenty of time for the planning and making of a wedding dress and all its trimmings, so that it may be enjoyed by the maker as well as the bride to be.

If the bride has strong ideas about the style of her dress it is best to design the dress first and then decide on the accessories like veil and flowers, bag and shoes. Occasionally, the dress may be designed around a particular accessory or piece of jewellery which is to be worn.

The placing of any detailed work on a wedding dress should be arranged so that it is seen to its best advantage. A bride will have her back to the congregation during most of a church service and dresses are often designed with this in mind, with a design feature on the back. However, if a long and elaborate veil is to be worn, any fine detail may be hidden by it, so remember this when planning the whole outfit.

115 Design for a wedding dress by Angela Dewar, making using of old Maltese lace.

118

Pay special attention to fastenings. These are often made into a design detail, as a long row of tiny covered buttons with rouleaux loops. The absence of a zip means that it is impossible to get the fastening jammed, in the excitement of getting dressed for the occasion!

A really good fit is absolutely essential and the first step is to make up a toile, whether a commercial pattern is being used or a specially designed one. For the toile, use a cheap fabric such as calico, mull, lining taffeta or even an old sheet. If a lining fabric is used, it may be possible to use it as the lining for the dress afterwards. The toile fabric should represent the weight of the chosen fabric of the dress, whether it is silk, cotton or a heavier type, such as velvet or heavy satin.

When choosing the material for the dress itself, remember that natural fibres make up into fabrics which are easier to handle than man-made ones and that synthetic fabrics tend to attract dirt and dust. The last point is important when working with white or light-coloured materials. Suitable storage of the gown, while it is being made, is sometimes one of the most difficult problems. When the toile has been perfectly fitted, it is time for the final decisions about any embroidery which is planned. This must be discussed with the bride, as she should feel as relaxed and happy about her dress as possible.

Once the amount and type of embroidery have been decided upon, the order of work must be thoroughly planned. It may well be that part of the fabric should be embroidered before the dress is cut out. This is often the case when tucks are being used. The same may apply to machine-embroidered edges. Other embroidery should be done after cutting but before the dress pieces are sewn together, as it is much easier to work on flat sections. When working with a large amount and sometimes heavy quantity of white or light material, the less it is handled the better. If a small amount can be taken to the machine at one time, it is easier to keep it all clean.

It always seems a pity that a wedding dress is usually worn only once, bearing in mind all the care and expense involved in its creation. It is surprising that it is not more often made in two parts, a blouse and skirt, or even three parts, blouse, skirt and train. The top will always serve as a lovely evening blouse, worn with a different skirt or with the original one, altered or shortened if necessary. For this reason, the outfit in figure

116 Detail of Maltese lace, showing the leaf motif which was used in figure 115.

115 was made up as a blouse, skirt and separate train.

The marriage of the Prince and Princess of Wales in 1981 was an influence which is still obvious in present bridal fashion, particularly in the use of antique lace combined with silk fabric. If old lace is to be used, care should be taken to find the correct shade of off-white or cream for the dress, as old lace is very seldom pure white.

When designing the embroidery for the bride's outfit in figure 115, a small leaf-like motif (*116*) from the old Maltese lace was re-interpreted in raised chain band and bullion knots, placed between the tucks on the bodice (*117*). A matching silk fabric was used for the outfit and the embroidery was stitched with a medium weight, silk twist thread. All the garments were sewn together with a silk sewing thread.

It is a pity to cut up antique lace and so the garments were designed around the pieces available, which were a yoke, cuffs and a long sash. Because the lace cuffs were too large for the wrist of the bride, it was decided to use them as a deep flounce on the sleeves, which are elbow-length. This shorter sleeve is flattering to the fore-arm and hand. The long piece of lace was used as the centre panel of the separate train. To give this panel an integrated look, hand embroidery was

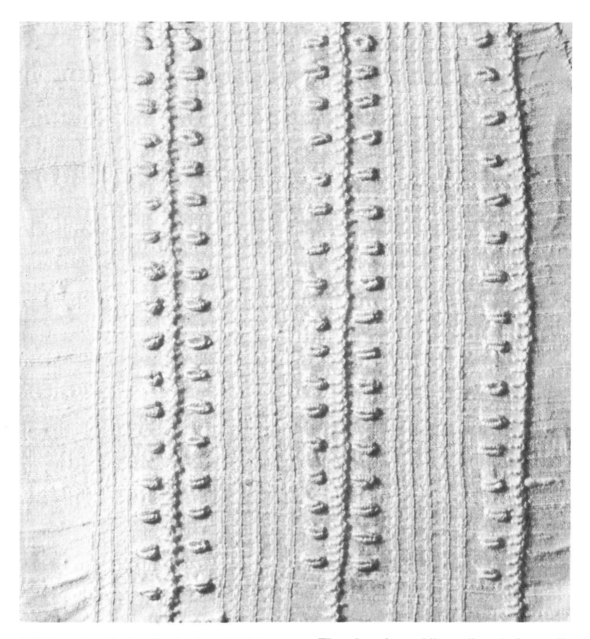

117 Embroidered leaf motifs taken from old Maltese lace and set between twin-needle tucks. Raised chain band and bullion knots.

added to each side of the lace on the silk fabric, also emphasizing the scalloped edges of the lace. This embroidery was worked in crested chain stitch and detached chain stitch. (*118*) A plain, cream silk tulle veil was worn, so that the embroidered details could be seen underneath.

The edge of a wedding veil made from tulle may very easily be decorated with the automatic scallop stitch on a modern sewing machine. This will give a pretty finish to an otherwise simple veil (see page 38). If a more elaborate decoration is required, delicate designs may be worked on the machine (see page 54) or by hand. An exquisite example of a hand-embroidered, needlerun lace veil can be seen in figures 119 and 120. This was made by Mary Anderson, using motifs from the antique lace of the bride's gown as the design for

118 Detail of the centre panel of the train in figure
115. Hand embroidery was added to each side of the
lace, on the silk fabric, also emphasizing the scalloped
edge. Creste hain and detached chain stitches.

LEFT
119 A wedding veil of silk tulle, designed and made by Mary Anderson.

120 Detail of the wedding veil in figure 119. The veil took nine months to complete. The motif was taken from old lace, used on the wedding dress. Limerick lace requires a fluid line, rather than isolated motifs, as the drawn fabric fillings are worked first. Then, using a double thread, a continuous line is couched around the outlines, with as few stops and restarts as possible, especially on the edge. The surplus net is then trimmed from the edge of the work, to give the scalloped effect. The embroidery was worked in silk, numbers 130/3, 100/3 and 70/3, on silk net.

the veil. The veil is a long, oval piece of silk tulle, with the weight of the design becoming heavier towards the very back and remaining lighter around the face of the wearer.

Figures 121 and 123 show two different ideas for decorating a bridesmaid's dress. In figure 121, the decoration is limited to the deep, pointed waistband and the high, stand-up collar. The dress and band are both white and the piped edges and satin-stitched flowers are worked in pink. The flowers worn as a headdress are of a similar colour and shape.

Traditional smocking was chosen to decorate the dress in figure 123, which was designed for a very young bridesmaid. The outfit consists of a long, pale green, cotton print dress, with three-quarter length sleeves. The smocked, cotton voile overdress is in the style of a Victorian pinafore, with deep shoulder flounces edged with cotton lace. The smocking on the front and back panels was worked in shades of pale green.

When smocking on very fine fabrics, such as voile, georgette or chiffon, it is important to allow at least four times the finished width when calculating the amount of fabric required (see page 91).

This dress would be charming for a country wedding, especially if the bride also wore a gown with smocked decoration (*122*).

121 Design for a bridesmaid's dress, by Jennifer Stuart.

122 A smocked wedding dress in silk, with seed pearls. Designed by Anna Roose for Celtic Fringe.

Evening dress

Clothes for evening dress offer an enormous choice of decorative techniques. Most of the methods described in this book could be used and adapted in an imaginative way and often effectively combined. Machine embroidery worked over fabric painting, and beading and couching used to enrich a lace fabric, are just two examples of combined techniques particularly suitable for evening clothes.

Shiny fabrics such as satin are often used for evening dress, and these are especially effective when they are quilted, like the jacket in figure 124.

Appliqué cloak

Colour plate 5 shows a dramatic use of appliqué to decorate a black and red woollen cloak, which would be suitable for any special outdoor occasion, or for wearing to the theatre or to a dance, over a black or red evening dress. Very fine wool was chosen for both the cloak and the lining and the appliqué and trimmings are of a soft, red, washable kid. (See Suppliers', page 142.)

A cloak pattern with shaped shoulders, stand-up collar and fly-front opening was used.

The outside of the cloak was cut from a black wool fabric, and the lining from a red one. For the appliqué design, the collar, piping and link fastenings, two skins of soft, red gloving leather were used. (See Suppliers', page 142)

For easier working, choose a design which will happily divide into front and back parts without overlapping the shoulder seams. If the design crosses the shoulder seam, the cloak has to be machined together before the appliqué can be done. This will make applying the design very awkward as the whole cloak has to be handled from the start.

Make a paper mock-up of the appliqué design in full size. Cut out the cloak, according to the pattern instructions. Tack the shoulder seams together and lightly press them open.

It is very important that the design is applied in the most advantageous position. Sometimes 1 cm (3/8 in.) up or down can make the difference between a very successful garment and a mediocre one. To find the right place for the decoration, it is best to get a friend of a similar height to put the cloak on. Now, stand far enough away for the whole silhouette of the figure to be

123 A bridesmaid's dress in cotton voile, with traditional smocking. Designed by Rosie Kendall.

124 A quilted and beaded evening jacket, designed and made by Heather Mowbray.

125 Design for a patchwork evening coat, by Angela Dewar, to be made up entirely of silk patches, shading from light to dark tones towards the hem. The smaller patches of the yoke form a deep V.

126 An embroidered cotton evening shirt, designed and made by Sonja Moore, a statistician. The design is based on a series of interlocking statistical Normal curves, and the shaded areas indicate cumulative probability integrals. The details were traced directly onto a cotton shirt, and a variety of black threads was used, with French knots, and the front band is worked in a fine blanket stitch. The front panel is lined.

128

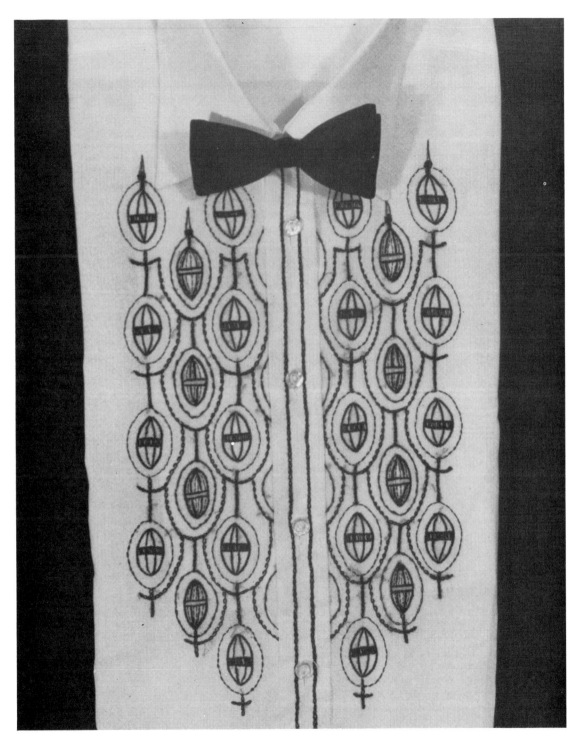

127 An embroidered cotton evening shirt, designed and made by Sonja Moore. The design is based on a Nash terrace in Regent's Park. The medallions are the 'pepperpots' of the roof, reflected across the balustrades, and swags link the pattern together. The details were traced directly onto the shirt and a variety of thread thicknesses was used. The stitches are chain and running stitch and the embroidered panel is lined.

seen. Pin the appliqué design onto the cloak. Step back again to check the position. Re-adjust and pin again until a well balanced appearance is achieved. Even if a design only goes across the top of a garment, or around the hem, it must be assessed from a distance so that its position can be judged in relationship to the whole project. Check and check again. This may seem very fussy, but it is impossible to take too much care at this point. When the best position is found secure the design with more pins. Now the cloak may be taken off the model.

Undo the tacking and spread the back and front parts of the cloak on a flat surface in order to work on them separately. Check the pinning of the appliqué design. Make sure that the paper motifs lie flat on the fabric. Should it pucker, it is better to correct the paper shape by folding or cutting rather than to change the layout, as this may upset the carefully worked out balance.

Mark the outlines of the whole design with tacking stitches as accurately as possible.

Take the paper mock-up off the fabric but make sure not to lose any of the alterations made.

Lay the paper mock-up onto the skin, with the right side of the design facing the wrong side of the leather, and draw the design onto the skin. Take care not to stretch the leather with the pencil or pen as this will result in a distorted shape.

Arrange the cut leather design onto the fabric. It should fit perfectly into the tacked-out spaces.

Most leathers show pin marks, so neither pinning nor tacking are suitable for keeping the motif in place during machining. A spray glue, used lightly, will do the job admirably. Larger motifs are difficult to glue all at once and are best done in sections as follows:

Cover all fabric and leather not to be sprayed with two large pieces of brown paper. Bring a small section of the leather design through between the two pieces of paper, fold it back and make sure that there is no gap between the two papers. Spray the glue onto the back of the leather, remove the paper, replace the sprayed section of leather onto its marked position and press it onto the fabric. Carry on to the next section of the design and glue in the same way, until the whole motif is in place. Take out all the tacking stitches. Stitch on the whole of the design by machine. On the cloak a red cotton/polyester thread was used, an ordinary needle no. 80 and a roller foot recommended by the machine manufacturer for working on leather and plastic. Talcum powder will sometimes help the leather to pass more easily under an ordinary foot; however, this is not to be recommended when using dark fabrics as the talcum powder is difficult to remove completely.

The outline of the design was stitched with a medium zigzag stitch with one stitch going through the leather and cloth and one just missing the leather and only piercing the cloth. The larger shapes were broken up with simple straight stitching echoing the outline.

When all the appliqué is done, the cloak was lined and finished off according to the pattern instructions. The cloak illustrated has red leather piping around its whole outer edge.

To prevent the cloak from slipping off the shoulders, link fastenings were put below both wrist points.

Four leather-bound buttonholes were worked near the outer edge, about 30 cm (12 in.) below the shoulder seam, on each side, front and back.

A link fastening, made up from two leather tassels joined by plaited thongs, holds the buttonholes together.

Holiday wear

For an expert dressmaker, a skiing holiday gives the opportunity to make a really unusual and attractive suit. In the bright light of a snowy landscape, brilliant colours can be used which would be out of place in another setting, and decorations can also be far more dramatic. Figure 128 shows a suit, made from a ready-quilted ciré fabric. The main part of the suit is white and the patchwork collar and appliqué on the back are in bright green and blue. The suit has a purchased gold piping trim around the zip fasteners, collar and the appliqué.

Patchwork, either used as appliqué or for making whole garments, is particularly suitable for casual wear, as it usually looks cheerful and light-hearted, rather than smart and sophisticated (129).

Figure 130 shows an exciting technique developed by students at Medway College of Design. Fur fabric was stitched closely by machine to create material of unusual texture and pattern. This was made into warm jackets, which are fun to wear and inexpensive to make.

128 A ski suit, designed and made by Sheenadh Martin. The suit is made from a ready-quilted ciré fabric with a patchwork collar and applied motif on the back.

129 A patchwork coat, designed and made by Ann
Dent. Varying sizes of log cabin patchwork squares
have been applied to a background of joined strips.

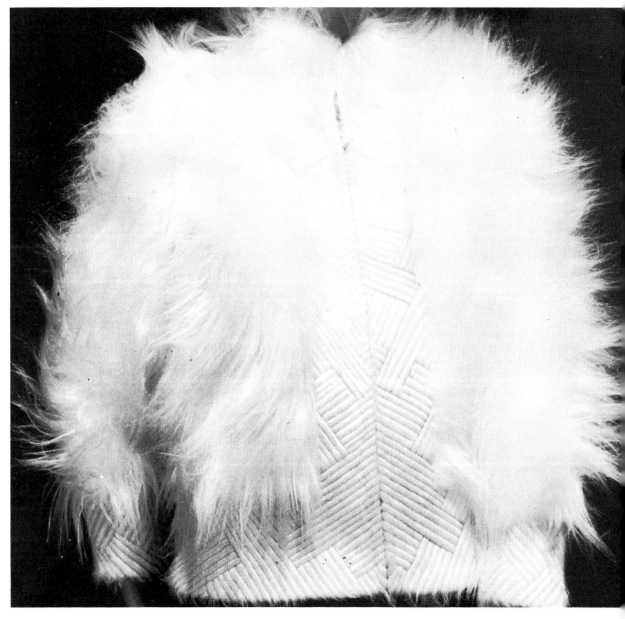

130 Borg fur fabric jacket, designed and made by
Debbie Davidson.

10 Embroidery on knitting

Knitted garments can be made more interesting by adding either texture or colour or both. Traditionally this is done during the knitting process. Texture can be created by using fashion yarns or complicated knitting stitches. Colour can be added in bands, in all over patterns or as motifs. These traditional methods require some skill and time.

It is easier, quicker and more economical to knit a plain garment in a plain yarn and to add the decoration afterwards in the form of embroidery. The garment may be knitted by hand or machine, or may even be purchased knitwear. An embroidered decoration will require much less yarn than a decoration which is knitted into a garment.

If a few rules are observed, the embroidery will become one with its knitted background, without making it unnecessarily thick or stiff.

Knitwear is so comfortable to wear because it is very elastic. It stretches in a horizontal direction, giving ease of movement, but stretches much less in a vertical direction, which makes it keep its shape and length. Any embroidery added to a fabric with these qualities must take on the same characteristics.

Overall patterns

The embroidery on a garment may be in the shape of an overall pattern (*131*). A plain pullover was knitted by hand, in a light blue double-knit wool. After the garment was completed the lower half of the front and back bodice and the sleeves were embroidered with detached chain stitches. A chunky, loosely twisted mohair/wool mixture in dark red was chosen for the embroidery. This yarn was much thicker than the knitting yarn, but very soft, so that it did not distort the even tension of the background knitting. The chain stitches were worked in one size and were arranged in chequerboard fashion, six knitting stitches and six knitting rows apart. Each chain stitch stretches over four rows of knitting. The working thread was kept loose, to give the chain stitches a plump and fluffy appearance. The rows of chain stitches were worked horizontally and in pairs, alternating the row after each chain stitch. In this all-over pattern, the working thread will lie in a zigzag line on the back of the knitting, allowing it to stretch in a horizontal direction, as it was able to do before any embroidery was added. If the distance from one chain stitch to the next is only small, the working thread may be stretched loosely along the back of the garment, but if the distance is longer than 2 cm (¾ in.), the working thread should be threaded through one or two knitted stitches, without letting it show on the right side of the knitting. This will help to keep the embroidery thread in place and will avoid any damage to the garment in wear.

To make the correct placing of an overall pattern easier for the embroiderer, it is possible to work a purl stitch in even spacing when knitting the garment. This will be a guide for the embroidery and will, in due course, be covered by it. In the case of the pullover in figure 131 one purl was worked in every sixth stitch of every third knit row in the lower half of the bodice and sleeves of the pullover.

Motifs in Swiss darning

Logos or monograms are often embroidered onto knitted garments to give them a personal note. For this kind of small motif, Swiss darning is a most suitable technique. With the help of a tapestry needle, a layer of imitation knitting is worked in one or more contrasting colours over the original stocking stitch. Swiss darning is best worked into a loosely knitted garment, using a soft working thread, either of the same thickness or slightly thicker than the knitting yarn. Care must be taken not to pull the working thread too tight. The embroidery should cover the knitting without puckering or pulling the background.

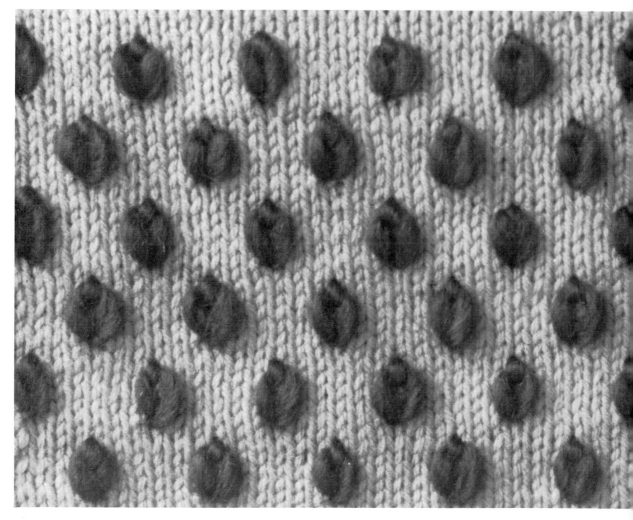

131 Stocking stitch pattern, hand knitted in a double knit yarn, embroidered with detached chain stitch in a chunky, soft mohair and wool mixture.

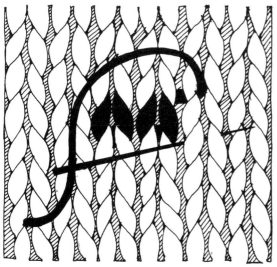

132 Swiss darning.

LEFT
133 The letter A, worked in Swiss darning, using chunky, soft mohair and wool mixture on a hand-knitted background in a smooth, chunky yarn and in stocking stitch pattern.

BELOW LEFT
134 The letter M worked in Swiss darning in a light coloured, double-knit yarn, on a hand-knitted background in stocking stitch pattern. The yarns for knitting and embroidery are the same, the background being a darker colour.

Embroidered bands

Some embroidery stitches, especially those based on a chevron, have enough natural elasticity to make them suitable for working in horizontal bands on knitting without tightening the garment.

In figure 135 three embroidery stitches are shown – chevron stitch, herringbone stitch and cretan stitch. It is not the aim of this kind of embroidery to cover up the background knitting, but only to add pattern, colour and texture. It leaves the embroiderer free to use yarns of any thickness or texture, from very fine to chunky.

Smocking

Smocking is an embroidery technique which is usually applied to woven fabric, but because of its elasticity, it is suitable for working onto a knitted background. Smocking stitches are usually worked onto a fabric which has been gathered tightly into tubes. (See page 91.)

A knitted background can have the 'tubes' knitted into it. When knit and purl stitches are alternated in a rhythmical pattern, vertical ribs are created which can be used as 'tubes' for smocking.

A very simple example is shown in figure 136. The basic knitting pattern chosen was:

*1st row K1, P2, K1, P2
2nd row P1, K2, P1, K2*
Repeat from*

The vertical ribs of K1 and P2 in between were treated as the tubes on a gathered fabric and surface honeycomb stitch was worked over them.

Knitting patterns with K2, P3, or similar make larger ribs and give scope for larger scale smocking. The scale of the finished garment must

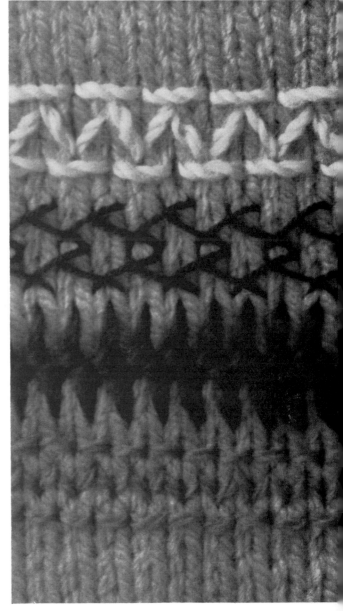

135 Hand-knitted stocking stitch pattern, embroidered with various yarns. The following embroidery stitches were used, starting from the top:

(a) Chevron stitch over two knitting stitches, and four knitting rows high.

(b) Herringbone stitch in two rows, each one three knitting rows high.

(c) Cretan stitch, one knitting stitch apart and six knitting rows high.

(d) Chevron stitch over one knitting stitch and four knitting rows high.

be kept in mind when deciding on the size of the smocking. Very large stitches look clumsy and contrived.

Figure 137 shows a larger rib pattern:

*1st row P2, K3, P2, K3
 2nd row K2, P3, K2, P3*
Repeat from*

On this example, after the knitting was completed, the ribs of K3 were gathered together in smocking fashion in the honeycomb pattern, ten knitting rows apart. The smocking was done with the same knitting yarn. Bugle beads were sewn over the smocking afterwards. The beads were sewn on with a cotton/polyester thread.

If a knitted fabric is to be manipulated, as in smocking, it is best to embroider with the same yarn that was used for the knitting, especially if it was wool. Any other thread may be too hard and, if pulled tight, may cut into the knitting. If, as in the example above, the yarn is too thick to pass through small beads, they should be sewn on separately and there should be no stress on the sewing thread, apart from holding the beads in place.

Threaded ribbons and cords

It is relatively easy to knit holes into an otherwise plain piece of knitting. These holes may be further decorated with ribbons or cords. Figure 138 shows a design for a pullover, knitted in mohair/wool mixture. Parallel rows of holes were knitted into the background. Some of the rows of holes had 0.5 cm (¼ in.) wide ribbon threaded through, which finished in a bow, others were laced up with a narrower ribbon. Note how the rows of holes are threaded and laced in a vertical direction only. Ribbons and cords are not elastic and would restrict the expected give of a knitted garment very much if applied in a horizontal line. Only when the ribbons are threaded in very loosely or in a zigzag line should they be used horizontally, as this gives enough play and stretch to allow the wearer to move freely.

Ribbons and cords should always be tested for colour fastness before they are applied to any garment.

Traditional knitting patterns such as Aran and Shetland are based on complicated cable and blackberry stitches, creating rich and varied textures. Garments in these styles are usually worked in one colour only, often in natural coloured wool or wool mixtures. In contrast, garments knitted in the Fair Isles are decorated with colour only, arranged in patterned, horizontal bands. A happy combination of the two styles can be achieved easily by knitting a textured garment and adding colour with embroidery. It is challenging to find different ways to link the knitted texture with the coloured embroidery. Figure 139 shows a knitted background of a simple texture of a diamond pattern with two parallel rows of holes in the lower half. The upper half is embroidered with flower heads in detached chain stitch and French knots. The stem is worked, appropriately, in stem stitch. It extends from the flower heads into the lower half of the diamond shape and turns the knitted rows of holes into leaves, belonging to the embroidered flowers. In this way, the knitted texture and the embroidered colour have become one design.

SUPPLIERS' LIST

UK

Beads
The Bead Shop
Neal Street
London WC2

Elles and Ferrier
Princes Street
London W1

Bobbin tape (for lace making)
Sebalace
76 Main Street
Addingham
Ilkley
West Yorkshire

Dress fabrics
John Lewis
Oxford Street
London W1

Liberty & Co
Regent Street
London W1

McCulloch & Wallace
25-6 Dering Street
London W1

Fabric transfer paints
Lowe & Carr Ltd
Instock Warehouse
Coniston Avenue
Leicester

Leather
John P Milner Leathers
Cilycwm
Llandovery
Dyfed

Silk tulle
Romance Bridals Ltd
12 D'Arblay Street
London W1

Threads
de Denne Ltd
159/161 Kenton Road
Kenton
Harrow
Middlesex

Mace & Nairn
89 Crane Street
Salisbury
Wiltshire

USA

Threads
Appleton Brothers of London
West Main Road
Little Compton
Rhode Island 02837

American Crewel Studio
Box 298 Boonton
New Jersey 07005

The Thread Shed
307 Freeport Road
Pittsburgh
Pennsylvania 15215

Canada

Threads
Sutton Yarns
2054 Yonge Street
Toronto
Ontario

Leonida Leatherdale
Embroidery Studio
90 East Gate
Winnipeg
Manitoba

BIBLIOGRAPHY

Butler, Anne, *Machine Stitches*, Batsford, 1976
Dean, Beryl, *Creative Appliqué*, Studio Vista, 1970
Gostelow, Mary, *The Cross Stitch Book*, Batsford, 1982
Green, Sylvia, *Canvas Embroidery for Beginners*, Studio Vista, 1970
Gutcheon, Beth, *The Perfect Patchwork Primer*, Penguin
McNeill, Moyra, *Pulled Thread*, Mills and Boon, 1971

Marshall, Beverley, *Smocks and Smocking*, Alphabooks
Nordfors, Jill, *Needlelace and Needleweaving*, Studio Vista, 1974
Puls, Herta, *Cutwork and Appliqué*, Batsford, 1978
Short, Eirian, *Quilting*, Batsford, 1978
Snook, Barbara, *Embroidery Stitches*, Batsford, 1963

INDEX